Digital
Marketing in Asia

A Start-Up Guide for Search Engine Marketing in APAC

Rohan Yamagishi

Contents

Prologue: Why Asia? 5

Chapter 1: What is Search Engine Marketing? 8

Chapter 2: Multilingual SEM: How to Succeed 23

Chapter 3: A Global View of SEM 37

Chapter 4: The Chinese Online Market 46

Chapter 5: The Japanese Online Market 63

Chapter 6: The Korean Online Market 81

Chapter 7: The Russian Online Market 93

Chapter 8: Taiwan 109

Chapter 9: Hong Kong 117

Chapter 10: South East Asia 122

    10.1 - Singapore 122

    10.2 - Thailand 127

    10.3 - Vietnam 130

    10.4 – Indonesia 134

About Rohan Yamagishi 138

About Paul Tarpey (Translator and Editor) 138

About Info Cubic Japan 139

Why Asia?

Did you know approximately half of the world's Internet users reside in Asia? In 2011, 45% of the planet's online community was from Asia, and it has been estimated that in 2014, this figure will pass the 50% mark. Numerous companies are increasing their investments in Asian economies, and it's not just large corporations, but small and mid-sized businesses, too. In fact, it is becoming much more common to see Western companies with Asian language websites. By having an Asian language website, companies are able to market their business online in Asia via various channels, one of which is search engine marketing (SEM). SEM is a popular, global form of online marketing that many Western companies have started utilizing as a means of reaching customers in Asia.

Search engine marketing is actually one of the best ways to market a business, so much so that I would say successfully entering Asian online markets nowadays without SEM would be nearly impossible. Companies have realized this, and many have successfully ventured into Asia via this route. Overall, the growing markets in Asia and the ease of penetrating them online via SEM shows that Asia is a business opportunity many shouldn't ignore.

		Reference
Population	3,879,000,000	World Bank 2011
Internet population	1 billion	Internet World Stats 2011
Internet use	25.7%	
Scale of online advertising market	24.8 billion USD	GroupM
Asia-Pacific region's share of world's Internet population	44.8%	Internet World Stats 2011

+ 78% of Internet users in Asia are under 45 years of age (comScore).
+ In 2011, 52% of the world's broadband Internet use was in the Asia-Pacific region (IHS iSuppli).
+ 58.8% of Internet users in the Asia-Pacific region are male; 41.2% are female (GlobalWebIndex Wave 6).
+ The almost 25 billion USD spent on Internet marketing in the Asia-Pacific region in 2011 represents 29% of the world's online advertising. For every 1 USD spent on online advertising in the Asia-Pacific region there is an average return of 1.78 USD. This makes online advertising the most cost-effective form of advertising in Asia (Nielsen).
+ 60% of Internet users in the Asia-Pacific region check product reviews before making purchases. Breaking this down by country: Vietnam comes in first at 81%; China is second at 77%, and Thailand is third at 69% (Nielsen).

As Asian economies have grown during the last decade, so too has the infrastructure of Asia's Internet and online advertising market. Examining Internet usage as a point of reference, China's rate is 38%; Vietnam's rate is 34% (Vietnam Internet Network Information Center), and India's rate is 10.2% (Internet World Stats). When you compare these statistics to that of the rest of the developed world, it becomes clear that the Asian online market still has much room to grow.

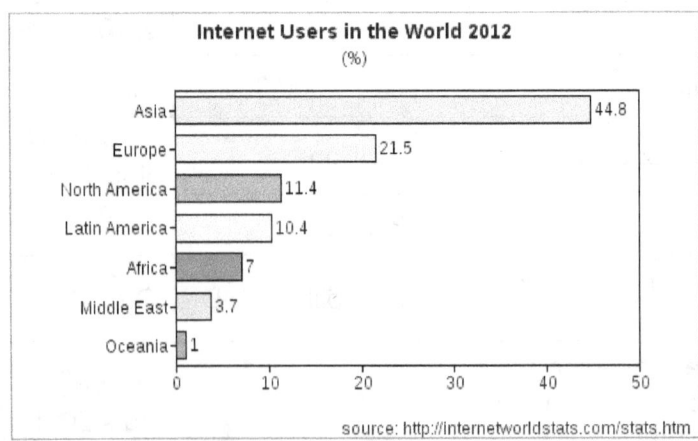

Fig A: Distribution of Internet users by world region

Most of the growth in Asia can be attributed to increases in Chinese Internet use, and since China's economy keeps expanding, its online population will continue to rise. Regional Internet expansion, however, is not limited to China. So, if you are considering promoting your business online in Asia, it is important to have an understanding of the makeup of online markets in different countries. Only then can you expect to find success entering Asian online markets.

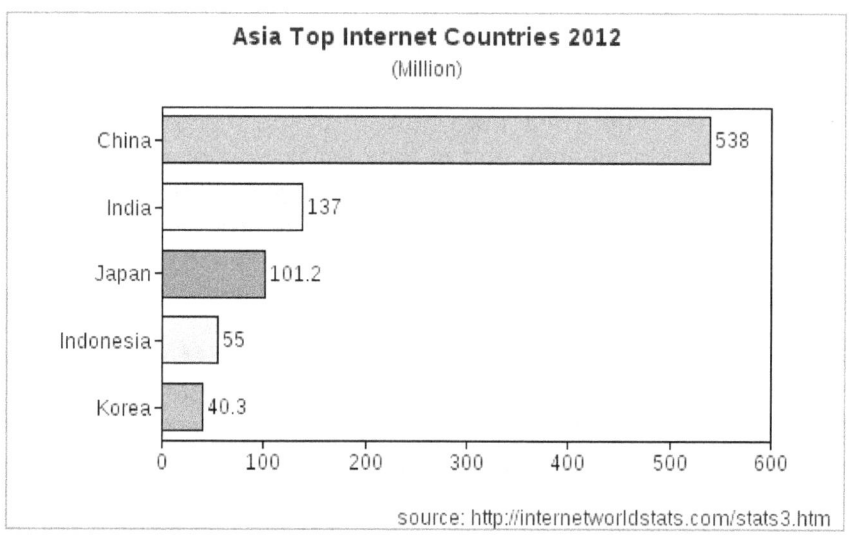

Fig B: Number of Internet users in Asia

India, which has the second highest number of Internet users in Asia, recorded 120,000,000 online participants in 2011. While this figure seems high, India could have an even larger Internet population as that figure represents only 10% of the country's population. Nonetheless, the number of Internet users is growing each year in India, and its online market, like China, will certainly grow in the future.

Given that India and China make up most of the Internet users in Asia and that each country is likely to add more participants well into the future, it is obvious that online business in these countries will only grow stronger. While India and China are the true giants of the Asian online market, the region combined is already the largest in the world and keeps on growing. It has definitely become a market that's capturing everyone's attention

What is Search Engine Marketing?

Search engine marketing (SEM) has become a globally popular Internet marketing channel within the last decade. The term "SEM" actually refers to two types of online marketing methods - search engine optimization (SEO) and pay-per-click advertising (PPC). While the SEM industry has already become a standard form of online marketing globally, it is still growing significantly and is forecast to continue doing so well into the future. The ease of penetrating foreign markets via SEM has allowed businesses and advertisers of various sizes to market online in multiple languages, which in turn has helped them conduct business across borders in ways that were simply not feasible before.

In this chapter, we will cover the basics of SEM, as a general understanding of it will be needed for later chapters. It was my goal to publish this book so that all types of people could learn the fundamentals of SEM, at the very least, so various basic SEM topics will be covered in this book. For those with a standing knowledge of SEM, the purpose of this book will most likely be to inform you of global trends and differences in SEM— especially for APAC—that you might not have been previously aware of. Regardless of prior knowledge, it is my hope that the information I have provided herein will help you get started with your global online marketing.

What is PPC Advertising?

PPC advertising (also known as "paid search") is marketing through ads that appear in search engine results pages (SERPs), which are connected to the queries that search engine users look up. For example, if a user types in keywords related to hotels in Spain, ads about Spanish hotels will be shown in the SERPs, as it is logically presumed they have an interest in finding information about hotels in Spain.

Let's take a look at SEM spending around the world, for now the country of Japan, which is my home country and one with a large SEM market. Japan's online advertising market in 2011 was valued at $7.6 billion, and as much as $2.6 billion was attributed to SEM. That's a large percentage. Comparing these figures to data from 2007, we can see that there has been an approximate 180% increase in SEM spending. Japan is not alone in this trend, though; SEM spending has been increasing in Asia and across the world. It's definitely an advertising channel that many simply cannot ignore.

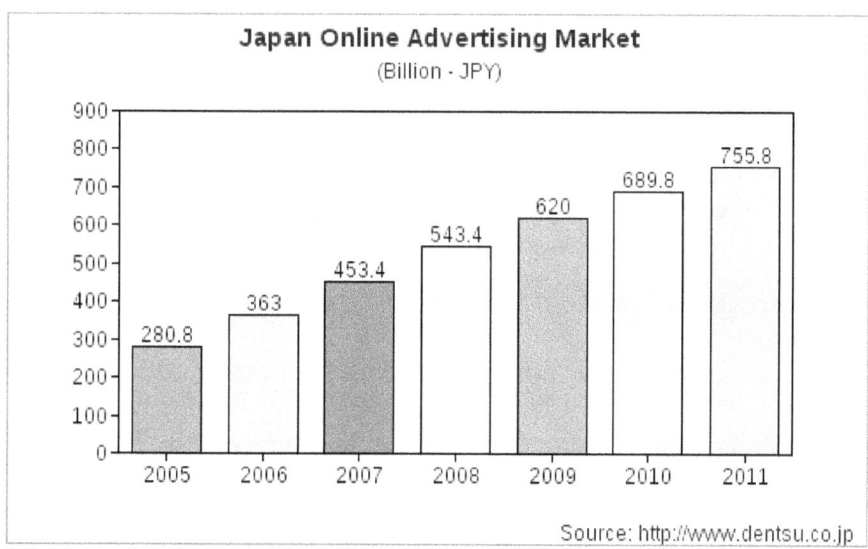

Fig 1.1: The change in size of Japan's Internet advertising market

PPC Ads
PPC ads are essentially text-based ads deriving from queries of search engine users. For example, if a searcher is interested in finding information about sporting goods, he might search for the keyword "sports equipment." This will bring up ads across the SERPs which are related to the keyword "sports equipment." The great thing about PPC advertising is it communicates directly to consumers by offering content specifically connected to their wants or needs. Since most Internet users access search engines on a regular basis, PPC ads can have a remarkably extensive reach, which is another of its attractive characteristics.

PPC Ad Bidding System

Most search ads adhere to a pay-per-click type system. This means advertising is free until an ad is clicked. Google, the world's most-used search engine, provides users worldwide keyword search volume data so that businesses and advertisers can research roughly how much it will cost to advertise a product or service. This is another great feature of PPC ads and facilitates the efficient planning of budgets.

Factors Determining Ad Rank

PPC ads can appear in a variety of positions, which is due to various factors, many of which are controllable. It is therefore important that you try to put yourself in a favorable position. The ranking system of PPC ads for many search engines around the world allows you to position yourself higher based upon your bid amount. Having a higher position leads to more clicks, naturally, and appearing lower has the opposite effect. The following formula explains this ranking system in a simple manner:

- *Ad rank = keyword bid amount X ad quality*

The bid amount is the money paid when an ad is clicked. This is decided by the keyword bid price designated by the advertiser and all the other bidders competing for the same keyword. Therefore, if someone outbids you on one of your keywords, there is a high chance his/her ad will appear higher than yours.

Ad quality, the other element of the formula, refers to the relevancy of the searched keyword to the content associated with your ad. The higher relevancy a searched keyword has to an ad, the higher quality it is said to possess. Specifically, the "quality" is determined by the click through rate (CTR) of your ad (generally more clicks are received for relevant ads), keyword and ad congruency, and the relevancy of the landing page's content to the ad. It is in this fashion that the bid amount and the quality of keywords are determined.

Keyword List Generation

Before running a paid search campaign, it is necessary to research what keywords are relevant to your business. The best way to start this process is to try using Google's free keyword tool, the Keyword

Planner. Using a multi-age apparel website as an example, if you were to develop a list of keywords, a great one to include would be "children's clothing." However, search engine users produce myriad queries for a single idea, so in order to ensure you cover as many of these searched terms as possible, it is best to use the Keyword Planner for reference. It will help you extract other related words that will assist you in developing a more thorough keyword list. For now, let's try "children's clothing."

Using these tools, you can extract other words related to "children's clothing," the word that is used in this example. Analyzing each relevant keyword's monthly search volume and competition, you can choose which ones would be best to add to your list in order to increase the reach of your business.

Keyword (by relevance)	Avg. monthly searches	Competition	Suggested bid
children wear	1,300	High	$0.51
childrens wear outlet	1,000	High	$0.48
designer childrens wear	210	High	$1.14
next childrens wear	210	Medium	$0.40
children s wear	10	Medium	$1.78
childrens wear digest	70	Medium	$0.11
childrens ski wear	1,000	High	$0.90

Fig 1.2: Many related keywords appear for the keyword "children's clothing"

The AdWords' Keyword Planner is a great tool to use as a first step in developing a strong keyword list. The total number of keywords contained in your registered list will depend on factors such as your industry or the conditions surrounding your business. One good thing is that there can be as little as one keyword to as many as thousands in your list; it really depends on you.

Creating Ad Copy

After you have created a keyword list, it is time to move on to writing your ad copy.

The actual length of your copy will depend upon which search engine advertising platform you use and its character limits, but the overall makeup of PPC ads is the same or similar to what is provided below. Google AdWords' ad specifications will be used for reference.

	Basic Character Limits	Character Limits for Select Countries (see below)
Ad Title	25 characters (1 byte) or 12 characters (2 bytes)	30 characters (1 byte) or 15 characters (2 bytes)
Ad Description: 1st Line	35 characters (1 byte) or 17 characters (2 bytes)	38 characters (1 byte) or 19 characters (2 bytes)
Ad Description: 2nd Line	35 characters (1 byte) or 17 characters (2 bytes)	38 characters (1 byte) or 19 characters (2 bytes)

Google AdWords allows extended length ad copies for certain countries. I have listed these for your reference:

Azerbaijan, Belarus, China, Hong Kong, Japan, Kazakhstan, Kyrgyzstan, Russia, South Korea, Taiwan, Tajikistan, Turkmenistan, Ukraine, and Uzbekistan.

Creating Effective Ads

For those of you who are just starting your paid search journey, I have decided to provide you some tips on ad creation. Catchy copy writing is not the only element that can be challenging when creating text ads; you will also need to fit everything into a limited space. The following tips for effective ad creation derive from data based on the analyses of 5,500 keywords (http://www.adgooroo.com/). Also, as this information is derived from English language sources, some elements might not apply to ad copy creation for other languages.

1. Enter target keywords into your ad's title
By entering the target keywords into your ad's title, the relevancy of your ad to the keyword search will increase, along with its CTR. When a keyword in your ad matches that which is searched, it will appear in bold lettering.

Used Car Classifieds
www.kbb.com/Used-Car-Classifieds
Large Inventory of **Used Cars** to Choose From. Search Now!
455,399 people +1'd or follow Kelley Blue Book

Fig 1.3: When the keyword "used car" is searched, it appears in bold

2. Enter specific prices into your ads
Certain sources claim that 15% of high performing ads list the price of the featured product/service. Usually the price of the advertised product/service is entered into the first description line of the ad (52%). The next most common place it appears is the second description line (39%) and lastly, the title (15%). While the inclusion of a price is not necessary for all types of business, if the price of the product/service advertised is especially economical or is essential to your sales strategy, it is generally good to include it in the copy.

3. Call to action
The call to action is a common phrase included in an ad that motivates viewers to perform a desired action. For example:

- "Get Your Quote Now."
- "Register in Under 1 Minute."
- "Find Out More Now."
- "Get Your Free Evaluation."
- "First 5 Customers Only -- Act Fast!"

These types of motivating phrases tend to increase the click through rates of PPC ads. 29% of ads include a call to action in the copy.

4. Use exclamation marks

Google AdWords allows the inclusion of exclamation marks to a certain extent. They aren't permitted in your ad's title, but they can be used conservatively in the descriptions. Research on this topic found that 34% of high performing ads include an exclamation mark, so there might be a correlation between it and increased CTRs.

5. Use of the trademark symbol

While it is not permissible to include a trademark sign (™, ©, ®) belonging to another company, it can be used for your own products if they are registered. It is recommended that you include trademark symbols wherever applicable, as users will trust your products more.

6. Enter specific numbers into your ads

According to research on PPC ad effectiveness, 41% of ads that perform well include some sort of numerical data. It is especially common to find this type of data in ads associated with e-commerce. While I naturally recommend including numerical data where applicable, I would warn against overuse, as it can lead to viewer confusion. It would be best to include one piece of numerical data as a standard. Consider the following examples:

- Hawaiian Vacation -- 45% Off!
- Kids' Clothing From $5
- SNS With Over 10,000,000 Users
- Brand-name Bags Under $300
- Over 100 Million Sold!

7. Inserting your brand's name

It is also smart to insert brand names when applicable, as they are trusted by many consumers and have been found to lead to more clicks. This is only recommended for companies or products that have established their brand, though, and shouldn't be used for branding purposes. Space is limited in PPC ads. So, for businesses just starting out, it would be best to use the space in your ads to include more information about your products/services. It is also important to note that using other companies' names or brands in your ads violates Google AdWords' advertising policy.

8. Try shorter length ads

In most cases, advertisers try to include as much information about their products/services as possible in their ads in order to use up all of the available space given to them. While this ideology allows for more information to be included, which can be a good thing, it doesn't help make the ad visually stand out from competitors. Creating shorter ads will attract more eyes, as it will appear different from most of those around them.

General length PPC ad:

New LCD TVs-Free Shipping
42" LCD TVs at Affordable Prices
Order Today & Same Day Shipping!

Short length PPC ad:

LCD TVs
42" Screens. Low Prices.
Free Shipping!

Even though the above ads contain nearly identical content, one conveys the information in fewer characters.

9. Use the term "free" with discretion

Adding the term "free" into your ad will increase its CTR, as research shows; however, the way it is integrated into the ad copy is important, as it is possible users are just curious about free offers and will click on your ad without any desire to purchase your product beforehand. Therefore, be specific about how you want to utilize the word "free" in your ads, all while thinking about how to reduce the amount of wasted clicks. 24% of ads that were deemed effective included the term "free".

10. Enter "www." into your display URLs

Looking at the data derived from 5,500 keyword searches, it was found that 80.6% of effective ads included a "www." in their display URLs. These types of ads were found to have higher CTRs than their counterparts.

11. "Official site"

When there are products or services that are advertised by different affiliates, sometimes the products/services' official website will appear lower in the SERP. If this is the case, then it is recommended the term "official site" be used in PPC ads to distinguish it from those of affiliates. The term cannot be used freely though - Google AdWords' policy only allows for truly official sites to use the term in their ads.

Developing an Effective Framework for Your Account

In countries other than the United States, Google AdWords might not control the top share of the search engine market. Other search engines lead the pack, and each has its own advertising; for instance, there is Baidu in China, Yandex in Russia, and Naver in South Korea. Regardless of which advertising medium you use for your paid search, it is important that your account be structured effectively. Luckily, all of the aforementioned search engines use the same three-tiered structure as Google AdWords.

The top tier of the structure is the **account** tier. At this level, you can manage the account advertising budget, e-mail addresses, and the account's notification settings, among other things. The first step to starting paid search advertising is to sign up for an account and adjust the account settings to your liking, such as those just mentioned.

The second tier of paid search advertising platforms is the **campaign** tier. It is here that you can adjust your campaign's daily budget settings, advertising region settings, advertising language, or the devices used for advertising (PC, tablet, or mobile). For example, if you plan on advertising on PC and mobile devices, you will need to designate how much of each campaign's budget you would like to allocate to each device. The more complex the campaign settings are, the more time-consuming the management of them will become. So, it is important to plan the structure of your campaigns well. If you are conducting SEM campaigns globally, there will be an even higher level of complexity, as you will have to balance advertising in different languages and regions.

The final tier of a paid search account is the **ad group** tier. Here, keywords and ads can be managed. In just one ad group you can register thousands of keywords and hundreds of ads. While it would be ideal to have a 1:1 ratio for ads and keywords, it is unrealistic. It is best practice then to have a well-developed list of related keywords uploaded into one ad group and include one to two ads that are associated with the overall essence of those keywords.

Display Advertising for Increasing Brand Awareness

Google AdWords not only offers advertising in the SERPs, it also provides a display advertising service. General search ads are text based and appear on the SERPs according to queries searched; display banners, on the other hand, are visual ads containing anything from images to words and appear in advertising spots on websites. Businesses that have signed an advertising contract with Google, such as blogs, news sites, portals, etc., allow display banner advertising on their pages through the AdWords platform. The actual time a user searches on Google is short compared to the time he or she spends browsing websites. The role that display ads serve is to advertise during this lengthier browsing time.

With Google's Display Planner, you are able to form display advertising plans via various criteria, such as interest, topic, keyword, or traditional individual site selection. The unique topic/interest feature of the Display Planner is a result of Google taking all of its partner sites and categorizing them by topic. For example, taking the category "travel," Google looked at all of its sites and grouped them around this topic. Advertisers can now advertise their travel banners on Google's travel-related partner sites in order to increase their CTRs and conversions.

For international SEM, it is a good idea to conduct search and display advertising at the same time, as certain data show it is more cost-effective than doing it separately. When running an online advertising campaign globally, you will need to increase your brand's awareness in order to hopefully increase sales. That is why display ads are very useful. If a consumer frequently sees display ads of your brand on sites he frequents, his awareness of your brand will increase, and he might be more likely to click the display ad or search for more information about your brand later on. There have been many companies who've actually increased their conversions through integrating display ads into their global search advertising campaigns.

Remarketing

Remarketing is also possible using display ads on Google. Remarketing is a process wherein the visitors to certain pages on your site are recorded and advertised via display ads on other sites they visit, all in hopes that they will come back to your site to make a purchase. This type of display advertising can be more effective, as it is based on specific user actions.

What is Search Engine Optimization?

Search engine optimization (SEO), simply stated, is both the internal and external process of modifying a website in order to increase its ranking in the SERPs. This involves things such as modifying the source code, adding text-based content, building a diverse backlink portfolio, and many other types of strategies. In this section, I will explain the various elements of SEO based on Google, as it is the most popular search engine in the world. SEO on other engines, such as Baidu, Naver, and Yandex, will also be discussed, but in later chapters.

SEO for Google

SEO for Google is the same in every country as long as you don't consider the differences in the timing of algorithm updates or the way Google processes languages other than English. Essentially, the importance of backlinks to your site and keyword insertion into your pages' meta tags is just as important in America as it is in other countries where Google is used.

Categorizing SEO at its highest level, there is **internal** SEO, whereby the source code and contents of a website are optimized, and **external** SEO, which involves various things, such as acquiring backlinks to a website from other sites. Both types of SEO need to be considered in order for there to exist the possibility of ranking higher in the SERPs.

Internal SEO

1. Title tag

The importance of your site's title tags for SEO is high. Title tags are important to different search engines all around the world, not just Google. For 1-byte language title tags, it is recommended to keep the tag to under 70 characters in length; for 2-byte languages, this figure drops down to 35 characters. When developing a title tag, at the very least the target keyword for the webpage should be inserted. It is also important to try to write your website's title tags in a way that is attractive to search engine users, so that they will want to click on your site. In the SEO industry, inserting keywords is standard protocol, so the real point to focus on is creating an attractive headline for your pages' title. If you are attempting SEO in foreign languages, it is recommended you have native speakers generate the copy, as it will ensure higher CTRs.

2. Description and keyword tags

The description and keyword tags are other important meta tags in your source code, just like the title tag. The description tag appears in search engine results, and it serves as an explanation of your site to search engine users. Regarding its length, up to 80 characters can be used for 2-byte languages, like Chinese or Japanese, but up to 160 characters can be used for 1-byte languages, such as English. The keyword tag, on the other hand, while still appearing in many websites, isn't used at all by Google in its search engine ranking algorithms. Its original purpose was to include keywords that are related to the content of each page of a website. This is not a necessary tag any longer for Google, but in terms of global SEO, such as on Baidu or Yandex, it is recommended to include it. Ideally, there should be 5-6 keywords per keyword tag.

In 2009, Google announced on their official blog that meta tags are not used at all in the determining of page rankings. Although they are supposedly not important for determining the ranking of pages on Google, for global SEO, which involves ranking on engines other than Google, it would be safest to include the aforementioned tags to ensure better chances of higher SERP rankings.

3. H tags

H tags are tags used for the subtitles found on web pages and are important for SEO. H tags can be used for different level subtitles and are written as: <h1>, <h2>, <h3>, etc. The <h1> tag is the top level tag and the most important. It is not necessary to insert all level H tags, but an <h1> tag should at least appear in your source code. It is in this tag that you will want to insert one of your target keywords.

4. Optimized content

Content optimization is another important aspect of SEO. Google and other search engines value high quality content and factor it in their ranking algorithms. No matter how much you try to optimize your site's mechanics, if you do not have compelling content, users will not stay on your site. Great content does not entail merely inserting keywords into your text; rather, it involves creating content that you feel a person will want to read and share with others.

Link Building

For Google and other search engines around the world, links are one of the most important factors in ranking websites. It is therefore important you have a strong portfolio of backlinks so that you can have a chance at ranking higher than your competitors. You must be careful though, as Google and other search engines are continually cracking down on sites that contain poor quality or irrelevant link portfolios. It is best to create an attractive site that will earn backlinks fairly on its own. Links posted via link building are eventually recognized as spam, and the result can lead to a huge drop in ranking or even being removed from the SERPs completely.

1. Blog links

In Asia, blog links are commonly used as a link-building strategy. This process involves having a blogger write about a business, product, or service and providing a link to the corresponding website. While there is no problem having an article written objectively by a blogger regarding a business, product, or service, paying him to have it written exactly to your liking is termed "stealth marketing," or marketed to people without their knowing it, and could be dangerous. It is good to exercise caution, as this can bring down your brand's image.

2. Press releases

Many companies are turning to press releases for their link building, as they can help increase the number of links to a website. These releases have two purposes -- news and SEO. Since press releases are often listed on news sites, they are also beneficial in that Google will crawl them faster (news sites are crawled more frequently than others).

3. Satellite sites

Satellite sites, or micro sites, are miniature sites made for the purpose of displaying content on a specific subject -- for example, a small site about used cars with lots of information on Hondas, Toyotas, etc. These sites can also be a tool used for SEO link building: they are very thematic in nature and are able to be paired with themes in another, main website. Linking between the two can improve backlink portfolios. What is ultimately important, though, is to create a satellite site not only for SEO purposes, but as a valuable addition to a main site.

4. Directory sites

Getting your site registered on high quality directory sites is also important for your SEO when you venture into new countries. For web marketing abroad, the first and foremost step is to get noticed by the most popular search engine in that country. In this case, a search engine directory would be a cost-effective approach to solving this problem. It actually is not just good for your site's SEO, but also as public relations for your website.

Differences between SEO & Pay-Per-Click Ads

As previously outlined, SEM is split into two groups: pay-per-click advertising and SEO. Each has its own pros and cons, of which you will need to fully understand if you are to be successful in your global online marketing. What is recommended when first starting a global SEM campaign is to start with pay-per-click advertising. One major reason is that you are going into uncharted territories, so you don't really know which set of foreign language keywords are optimal for you to advertise with. Paid search will allow you to experiment and change your strategies easier and faster than SEO does. This way, you are at least able to get to higher rankings faster than you would via SEO. Search engine optimization will take time to be effective, and you most likely won't be able to get to higher rankings in the SERPs as quickly as you could via pay-per-click advertising.

	SEO	**PPC**
Speed	After implementing your SEO strategies, it will take time for its effects to be felt. In some cases, it will only be a matter of days, but in others, it might be weeks or months.	By running PPC ads, you can gain almost instantaneous high rankings in the SERPs. It is an extremely effective way to start your global web marketing. Short-term campaigns can also be done easily via PPC advertising.
Rank	Ranking is something that is determined by each search engine's own ranking algorithms. Ranking is not something that can be guaranteed by any means. Also, with algorithm updates, there are cases in which websites' rankings change significantly.	Depending on the amount you bid per keyword, you will have the chance to control your ranking to a certain extent. While the quality of your site and ads is also a factor in ranking, the higher the bid, the higher the ranking is the norm.
Cost	SEO can cost you significantly to start, but afterward it is generally cheaper than your average paid search campaign. Sometimes link building can even be free.	The cost of advertising will only be as much as your allocated budget.

Multilingual SEM: How to Succeed

If you are thinking about starting a multilingual SEM campaign, you will need to prepare yourself much more than you would for any domestic marketing campaign you've done. Everything from technical SEM to the process of keyword selection and copywriting needs to be considered within the framework of the new country in which you will be marketing. In this chapter, I will go over the essential points to remember when conducting multilingual SEM so that you can start your venture off on the right path.

Fundamentals of Multilingual PPC Advertising

PPC advertising, or paid search, is a great form of online advertising to choose if you are considering marketing in foreign countries. Its foremost merit is that it makes reaching potential consumers easy and effective through the use of search engines as an advertising medium. As most of the online community across the world uses search engines on a regular basis, the reach that you can obtain via PPC advertising is significantly higher compared to other advertising platforms. Global paid search involves many languages, though, so if you want to reach consumers across the world, simple, direct keyword and ad copy translations will not suffice. This is one of the challenges you will face. Another challenge is that in other countries, there are unique paid search advertising platforms (e.g. Baidu in China, Naver in South Korea, and Yandex in Russia) that you will have to learn how to operate. In this chapter, I will provide you the knowhow needed in order to conduct multilingual, global PPC campaigns effectively. That way, it will be a fun, not stressful, experience.

Different Countries, Different Search Engines
The first step in starting a global paid search campaign is to research the different markets you're entering to find which search engine or engines command the top shares. Google is undoubtedly the leading

search engine in the world, which means it commands the highest share globally, but not every country follows suit. There are countries in the world in which advertising through Google AdWords won't provide you the reach you need to successfully market your business. I therefore recommended you look into the market share each search engine possesses in every country in which you plan to advertise. Luckily, you will find this information, for Asia, throughout the following chapters.

Differences in Language

One thing to be careful of when running a global paid search campaign is the differences in character limits for each country. In Asia, you have Japanese, Chinese, and Korean, which are 2-byte languages. This means that 2 bytes are required to display one character. English, on the other hand, needs only 1 byte. This means that languages like Japanese or Chinese are allowed fewer characters for their PPC ads when compared to the 1 byte languages like English, because each character uses more data.

Language and Regional Settings at the Campaign Level

It is very important to set up your multilingual PPC campaigns effectively. Google AdWords allows for campaign level language and regional settings to be made, so it is recommended you adjust according to your marketing situation. You should first ask yourself the following questions:

- Should I target a specific region?
- Should I target a specific language?

These two questions are necessary to ask yourself when formulating a global PPC campaign. When targeting foreign countries, such as Singapore or Hong Kong, for example, there can be multiple languages you need to consider. In the case of multiple languages, such as in these two nations, you can create campaigns and landing pages for each target language. Having both Chinese and English landing pages, along with their accompanying PPC campaign data in English and Chinese, will ensure more traffic reaches your site. On the other hand, if you just want to target one specific language, you can choose the whole world as your targeted region and reach speakers of that language across the globe. If you plan not to designate a specific service area, it is best to set the whole world as your advertising region.

1 Campaign, 1 Language Rule

When developing PPC campaigns, it is recommended you assign one language to each campaign. When naming these campaigns, make sure to include the language and

area so you can organize and operate them more effectively.

Example -- Campaign naming:

- Hong Kong (English)
- Hong Kong (Chinese)
- Mexico (Spanish)
- Spain (Spanish)

The structure you develop for your multilingual campaigns will greatly affect their overall performance. Constructing your account half-heartedly might lead to your not reaching the level of performance you were expecting, because the mere daily operation of your account will become an inefficient ordeal. If you are operating a large paid search account, you might want to consider splitting it into multiple accounts based upon language. This might end up being more convenient and effective, as you will be able to allocate and adjust your budgets better, and all the internal data will be unified by language. Matters such as these are truly decisions you need to make on a case-by-case basis. What is most important overall is to keep your campaigns' structure identical or similar to your company's website.

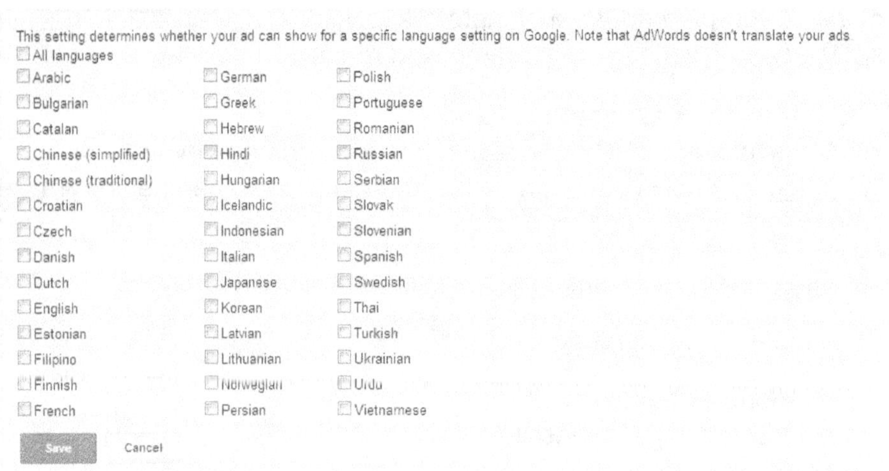

This setting determines whether your ad can show for a specific language setting on Google. Note that AdWords doesn't translate your ads.

☐ All languages

☐ Arabic	☐ German	☐ Polish
☐ Bulgarian	☐ Greek	☐ Portuguese
☐ Catalan	☐ Hebrew	☐ Romanian
☐ Chinese (simplified)	☐ Hindi	☐ Russian
☐ Chinese (traditional)	☐ Hungarian	☐ Serbian
☐ Croatian	☐ Icelandic	☐ Slovak
☐ Czech	☐ Indonesian	☐ Slovenian
☐ Danish	☐ Italian	☐ Spanish
☐ Dutch	☐ Japanese	☐ Swedish
☐ English	☐ Korean	☐ Thai
☐ Estonian	☐ Latvian	☐ Turkish
☐ Filipino	☐ Lithuanian	☐ Ukrainian
☐ Finnish	☐ Norwegian	☐ Urdu
☐ French	☐ Persian	☐ Vietnamese

Save   Cancel

Fig 2.1: The language settings screen. Currently there are 42 different languages available for Google AdWords.

Ad Group Creation

As explained above, it is ideal to assign each campaign just one language. Since ad groups are subsumed within campaigns, the same theory will apply to them. Although it is possible to apply numerous languages to ad groups, each ad group should ideally have the same language as its campaign.

Ideal Keyword Lists

In order to maximize your paid search performance, it is also necessary to optimally format your keyword lists. First and foremost, it is highly recommended you do not merely directly translate your English language keywords into the other languages in which you are marketing. Sometimes, a translation of your keyword will be accurate in the literal sense, but it isn't actually what is being searched for by users in the target language. For example, if you were to translate the phrase "search engine optimization" into French, you would get "l'optimisation des moteurs de recherché." While this makes sense literally, the word "Référencement" is the actual term that is used. Take a look at the following data, extracted using the AdWords Keyword Planner:

Keyword (by relevance)		Avg. monthly searches ?	Competition ?	Suggested bid ?
Référencement		6.600	High	$6.12
L'optimisation des moteurs de recherche		10	Low	-

Fig 2.2: Simple translations do not allow you to find the proper keywords.

When generating your global keyword lists, you will also need to consider including variations of each keyword. For example, there will be instances in which slang terms are searched for more than their dictionary entry counterparts. Also, there can exist differences in search volume depending on location. Taking the English language as an example, in America, "transportation" is the most searched term for finding different means of traveling from point A to point B, but in England, "transport" is preferred.

Keyword (by relevance)		Avg. monthly searches ?
transport		8.100
transportation		1.900

Fig 2.3: Search volumes for "transport" and "transportation" in England.

Keyword (by relevance)		Avg. monthly searches ?
transport		6.600
transportation		33.100

Fig 2.4: Search volumnes for "transport" and "transportation" in America.

Selecting the proper keywords for your different campaigns will ensure optimal performance. I firmly recommend you have a native speaker of the variety of language you are targeting develop your keyword lists or you use a multilingual SEM expert with experience in the targeted languages. The keyword lists that you upload into your account(s) are directly linked to the success of your PPC advertising campaigns. If you do not ensure accuracy and optimal reach via native speakers, you can end up incurring unnecessary costs, which will decrease your overall performance.

Ad Copy Structure

PPC ads for your global campaigns need to be written by people with copywriting experience. Words are limited in PPC ads, and there are competing advertisers to deal with, so you need to create ad copy that capture users' attention and makes them want to learn more about your product or service. Just by changing the way you use your words to convey a message, you can experience better results. Let's use an online shoe store as an example. This store normally sells their shoes for $100, but currently they are running a campaign that has reduced it to $50:

- "Shoes Normally $100, Now Only $50!"
- "$100 Shoes, Now 50% Off!

Both ads say the same thing, but certain users will construe them differently. In light of the above ads, the effect of a price can be more powerful than a percentage, or vice versa, depending on the country where you are advertising. This type of issue is something you have to consider though, especially when copywriting in multiple languages. For instance, areas other than price might be more effective to focus on, such as secure shipping, timely deliveries, or a flexible return policy.

The One Language Principle

When you run global paid search campaigns, it is highly recommended you unify your keywords, ads, and landing pages by using the same language. If a landing page is in a different language from its ads and keywords, your overall performance will take a hit. For instance, if a user clicks on an English language ad and is brought to a German language landing page, even if he is a speaker of both languages, he'll probably question the legitimacy of the site and/or business.

Advertising in Different Locations

Google AdWords allows advertisers to segment their targets by language or regional settings. The following items are the main criteria that Google uses to categorize different target segments:

1. Google domain display
If advertising in Japan using the Japanese language, ads will be shown on the domain www.google.co.jp. Moreover, when the advertising language is set to Japanese, ads will be shown to users whose personal Google search settings are set to Japanese.

2. IP address
IP address information will also be referred to Google to designate a region. For example, if you target Taiwanese consumers, search results will include users of www.google.com.tw as well as those who have a Taiwanese IP address and search on www.google.com.

3. Google account language
If a user possesses a Google account, he can set his main language for the account. If the set language is English, ads that are in English will be shown to the user.

Let's say an American hotel is trying to target users from Hong Kong and that both English and Chinese are used in the marketing campaign. The advertising location is Hong Kong, and the advertisements are in English and Chinese. While this would help extend one's advertising reach within Hong Kong, it wouldn't extend to Hong Kongese outside the country. Thus, when Hong Kongese are traveling abroad, say in America, and using their smart devices to make hotel reservations in the U.S., they will be disregarded if Hong Kong is the only designated advertising location. This shows you must consider all possibilities when designating your regional and language settings for your PPC campaigns.

Landing Page Settings

If you haven't created a landing page in the specific language you want to advertise in, you naturally do not want to run ads for that language. When developing or selecting landing pages, make sure they have corresponding ads in the same language that will guide users to them. If they are different, you risk losing conversions to confused users.

PPC Advertising = Marketing Research

When a business wants to promote its products or services overseas, they often do not know what country is best to target. For a case such as this, paid search can help you discover what locations will be most profitable. By setting the advertising regions to "all" and language to "English", users all around the world who search in English will be targeted. After a while, you will gather enough data to generate informative reports via Google AdWords' report feature, whereupon you can analyze the findings and discover which countries best meet your needs. You then can decide whether or not to stop advertising in countries with higher than ideal cost per acquisition (CPA). With real data, you will know which countries have the most demand for your products/services. Of course, you can initially find out how many potential consumers can be reached by just referring to Google's search volume data, but when it comes to the actual sales of your products/services, gathering real data on which countries are best is something that Google's numbers cannot tell you.

Multilingual PPC advertising requires much research and preparation before you actually start running campaigns. If you do it properly, though, and effectively operate your campaigns, PPC can be a very powerful advertising medium. Don't be afraid to fail, though, as trial and error is an important part of the paid search advertising process.

Basics of Multilingual SEO

There are three important points to remember about global SEO:

- Ensure proper regional targeting.
- Develop content strategies for each advertising language.
- Plan link-building strategies for each country in which you advertise.

Proper Regional Targeting

For multilingual SEO, properly setting your target regions is an important matter. When performing SEO on a website with multiple languages, it is important to not only have a solid internal and external SEO strategy, you also need to properly target your advertising region; otherwise, your work will be pointless. The search engines, Google and Bing, base their targeting on multiple information sources, some of which I will share with you in this section.

1. IP Address Information
Most search engines use websites' hosting locations (IP address information) to classify their regional settings. This means that for sites hosted in Mexico, Spanish content would be expected to be found on the site, while sites hosted in Italy would feature Italian content. To use Italy as an example, this means hosting a site in Italy is the best choice for Italian SEO. However, when marketing globally, the location of a business office and the location of its hosting site are probably in completely different areas. If a business has a global site, it would be difficult to have different hosting servers for each language, so it is ultimately unrealistic to think search engines only designate a site's location based on where it's hosted. If you think about this issue from the perspective of a user, a business hosting its site in the same country will help to increase its access speed (countries with poor internet infrastructure excluded). As such, search engines do not use only this piece of information for determining location. In reality, search engines choose to refer to multiple pieces of information to determine the target region of a website.

2. Country Code Top Level Domain
Country code top level domain (ccTLD) is a rather influential factor for search engines in determining a website's target region. The ccTLD is indicated by the letters appearing to the right of a URL: for example, "fr" is the ccTLD in www.yourdomain.fr.

The "fr" indicates that it is a French website, and the "sg" in www.yourdomain.sg shows it is a Singaporean site. Of course, if the URL is www.yourdomain.sg, we can expect that its owners are targeting Singapore. Thus, with a ccTLD, it is easy to designate a region, and search engines use it as a clear indicator for their targeting. However, a ccTLD cannot tell whether the website's owner is incorporated or conducting business in the same country. Regarding using ccTLDs from the perspective of SEO, it is best to consider it on a case-by-case basis. The problem with acquiring a new ccTLD domain is that there are no backlinks directed toward it. When you acquire a new domain, you can naturally expect that it will take time to move up in the SERPs without a history of backlinks. Also, while a ccTLD does help to designate a region, it doesn't seem to have a direct connection to helping improve your ranking. (Search engines have stated that ccTLDs aren't considered in terms of ranking). With regard to areas other than SEO, ccTLDs do have their merits. For example, a ccTLD gives visitors a sense of trust, as it is an indicator that the business is local. It's probably safe to say most consumers are more comfortable purchasing items from a site in their own country than a site located in a foreign one. Overall, it is up to you to consider whether acquiring a new ccTLD is beneficial or not.

Generic top level domain (gLTD)	.com, .net, .org, .biz, .info, etc.
Country code top level domain (ccTLD)	.jp (Japan), .de (Germany), .fr (France), .tw (Taiwan)

3. Website Language and Content
Search engines use the language and content of a website as one piece of information in classifying its location. For example, the Russian search engine, Yandex, indexes pages in Russian and English, but Japanese or Chinese pages are not indexed much at all. Information, such as phone numbers or addresses, is also used to determine target region; these items are weak indicators though. Also, you can determine the country or region of a page just by the language in which it is written.

4. Google Webmaster Tools for Regional Targeting
Google's Webmaster Tools allows users to easily perform regional targeting for their website. This feature also allows regional targeting for cases in which the folders or subdomains of a single website are isolated by language. While this feature is normally convenient, it can only be used with generic domains, such as .com, .org, .net, etc.

5. Regional targeting with Meta Tags
It is also possible to use meta tags to designate location. Currently, Google does not use meta tags for distinguishing a site's region, but for other search engines, like Microsoft's Bing, which does not have a regional targeting feature, it is possible.

<meta http-equiv="content-language" content="XX">

Code	Language
BG	Bulgarian
CS	Czech
DA	Danish
DE	German
EL	Greek
EN	English
EN-GB	English-Great Britain
EN-US	English-United States
ES	Spanish
ES-ES	Spanish-Spain
FI	Finnish
FR	French
FR-CA	French-Quebec
FR-FR	French-France
HR	Croatian
IT	Italian
JA	Japanese
KO	Korean
NL	Dutch
NO	Norwegian
PL	Polish
PT	Portuguese
RU	Russian
SV	Swedish
ZH	Chinese

Search engines use various forms of information, as outlined above, to perform their location targeting. Since each search engine has its own unique indicators for targeting, it is not certain which indicators are the most influential. Therefore, you will need to perform your SEO in light of each search engine's own targeting variables.

Separating Site Maps by Language

Currently, site maps are supported by many search engines. By setting your site map, you can identify search engine crawling errors, so this is a great feature for SEO. If your content is displayed in many languages, you can make site maps for each language, such as:

- http://www.example.com/VN/sitemap.xml
- http://www.example.com/JP/sitemap.xml
- http://www.example.com/UK/sitemap.xml

Multilingual Content Strategies

It is crucial that you have a well-developed content strategy for your global SEO. Just focusing on the technical aspects of SEO is not enough to be successful on the worldwide stage. Though many individuals look to extensive link building measures for their SEO, as it was successful in the past, many companies have shifted their focus to quality content. When creating content for your SEO, you'll need to consider how best to insert your target keywords on top of producing quality content. For global SEO, since you will be dealing with multiple languages, mere translations of your original text will not suffice. Help from people with multilingual SEO content writing experience is recommended. What is important overall is that you research what level of content you will need for SEO in different languages and make sure to have native speakers write it for you. If this is difficult to do in-house, outsourcing is a viable alternative.

Beware of Duplicate Content

For multilingual SEO, sometimes people target multiple locations with one language. A good example of this is targeting the United Kingdom and America using the English language. English is pretty much the same worldwide, save for differences in vocabulary, pronunciation, and colloquial phrasing, so you would think it was OK to use the same content worldwide. This is not a good idea, though, as it can lead to the possibility of search engines penalizing you for duplicate content, which can actually lead to your being removed from search engine indices. It is recommended that you change content for each target region, even if it is the same language, because there is always the possibility of being removed from a search engine's index.

Regional Link Building

SEO on search engines other than Google (Baidu, Yandex, Bing, etc.) also requires strategic link building. For countries that still have underdeveloped SEM industries, you can expect that there are fewer businesses doing SEO, and, thus, it will be easier for you to rank higher in the SERPs. This is changing each year, though, so it is important to develop a solid strategy early on. Multilingual link building strategies involve getting links from sites all in the same language. While in the past, it was possible to increase your Chinese SERP rank via English language site backlinks containing Chinese keywords, this has changed. Now these types of links are considered spam.

Handling Google

Currently, Google is the most used search engine in the world. This means that for global SEM, you will have to perform SEO in light of Google in most cases. Google fundamentally seems to handle the world's myriad languages in the same fashion, but, of course, there are certain algorithms that need to be implemented in order to process languages that are different from English. In terms of ranking, though, Google seems to treat variables in the same way even across borders. For example, if you consider how Google handles backlinks, results seem to be the same in Japan, America, Vietnam, Germany, or pretty much anywhere Google is accessed. Google's algorithm updates start in America (in the English language), so Penguin and Panda will be felt first in the U.S. and then in other locations across the globe. This means that there is a time delay between the initial update in English and the subsequent updates in other languages. It is therefore possible for certain non-English SEOs to foresee what changes will come and develop a strategy to handle it.

SEO for Bing

SEO for Bing seems to mirror that of Google, meaning things like site content and backlinks are treated in the same manner. It is difficult to measure the differences, though, as there is not much information on Bing available in the SEO industry due to its smaller share of the market. However, this might be changing, at least for the Asia-Pacific region, as Yahoo Taiwan and Hong Kong both have replaced their search engines with Bing. This has given the search engine a more influential role in the area. Here I will provide some general guidelines for SEO on Bing:

1. CTR is important

Bing appears to value the CTR of sites when ranking. This means the more a site is clicked, the better chance it has at moving up in the SERPs. What is recommended then, is making sure your site's meta data that appears in the SERPs, such as your title and description tags, do not just contain target keywords, but also effective copywriting that attracts more users to click on your site.

2. Bing Webmaster Tools

Bing has its own unique version of Webmaster Tools that you can take advantage of. Using Bing Webmaster Tools, you will be able to get useful information for your site's SEO, such as how to apply for URL indexation, sitemap settings, number of indexes, etc. You can find Bing's Webmaster Tools program via the following link:

- http://www.bing.com/toolbox/webmaster/

3. Content really matters

Since Google's last update, websites with especially poor content or overall poor usability have been removed from Google's index at a higher rate than before. However, this trend is not limited to Google; it is also occurring on other search engines like Bing. That's why it is imperative you not only go about your link building strategies in the proper manner, but also produce high quality content if you want to succeed at global SEO.

Different Countries, Different SEO Challenges

The level of difficulty for SEO can change drastically from country to country. For example, in South Korea, where Naver is the main search engine, SEO is not even worth the effort as only three sites appear in the first page of organic results. For other countries' search engines though, such as Russia's Yandex, there are existing link building markets. In these countries, links are still an important part of SEO. In this respect, for different search engines, there are different SEO strategies that you have to implement. For Asia, which isn't dominated by Google as the rest of the world is, it is imperative you gain an understanding of the different search engines that are in use and how to perform SEO on them, if you wish to market successfully online in the region.

A Global View of SEM

This chapter will focus on SEM shares and the fundamentals of search engine marketing, all in light of global online marketing. In order to successfully conduct SEM in different countries or regions of the world, different sets of knowledge of the markets are required. In this chapter, I will provide data to assist you in becoming more effective in the world of global SEM, particularly for Asia.

World Advertising Expenditure by Medium

According to a 2012 Nielsen study, there was a 12.1% change in online advertisement spending when compared to 2011, which made it the only advertising form that surpassed 10% growth. Digging deeper and looking at the numbers by region, the Middle East and Africa increased by 35.2%, South America by 31.8%, and the European Union by 12.1%. While Africa and South America's overall expenditure is still at a relatively small scale, the two regions saw significant increases in online advertising budgets. This and other data shows that in almost every continent Internet marketing is becoming an ever more indispensable form of advertising.

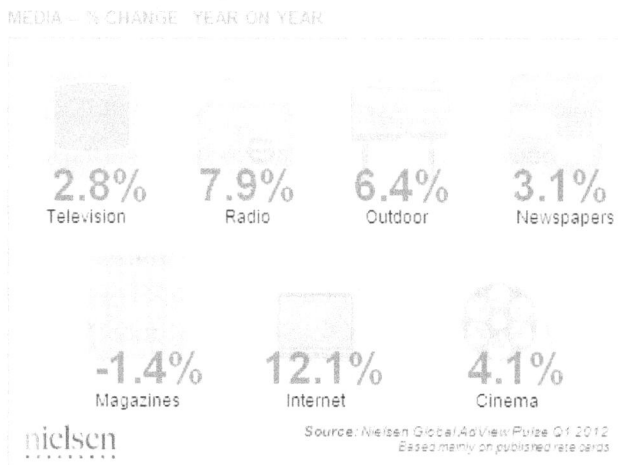

Fig 3.1: Online advertising expenditure was the only medium to pass the 10% mark.

Online Advertisement Expenditures around the World

First, let's look at the overall world online advertising market. Currently, the world market is valued at 94.2 billion USD and is expected to grow to 132.1 billion USD by 2015. Forecasters predict that growth will continue at an annual rate of at least 10% in the near future

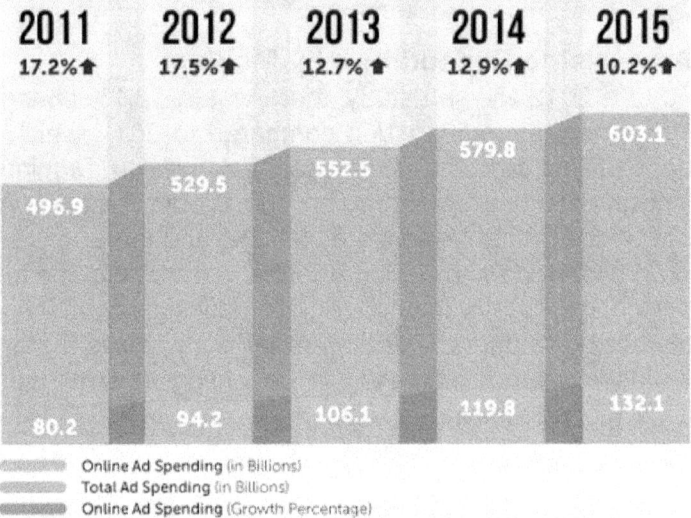

Fig 3.2: Global online advertising is expected to increase into the future.
Source: http://www.go-gulf.com/

When looking at global Internet advertising shares, Google, Yahoo!, Microsoft, and other search engines command more than 56.4% of the total market. From Asia to many other nations and regions across the globe, budgets for search engine advertising are increasing significantly.

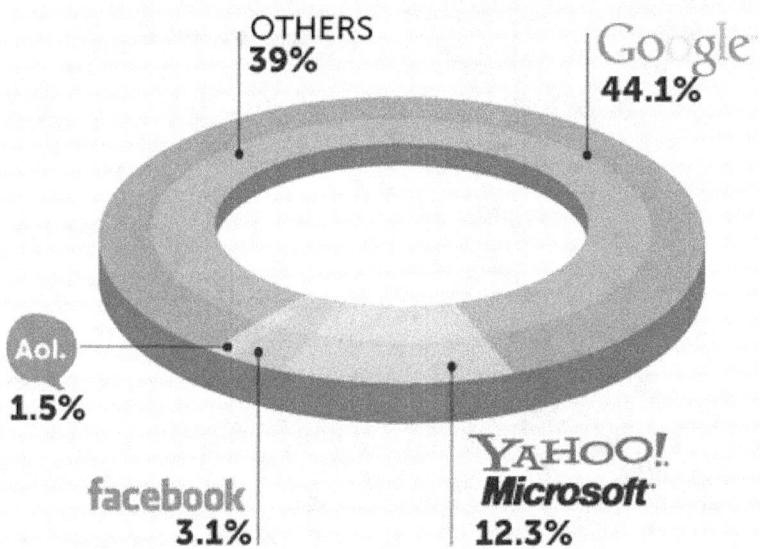

Fig 3.3: 44.1% of the world's online advertising market share is dominated by Google.
Source: http://www.go-gulf.com/

What's more, when comparing different advertising media, it becomes apparent that search network PPC advertising is the most popular form: 49% of online spending goes to this format.

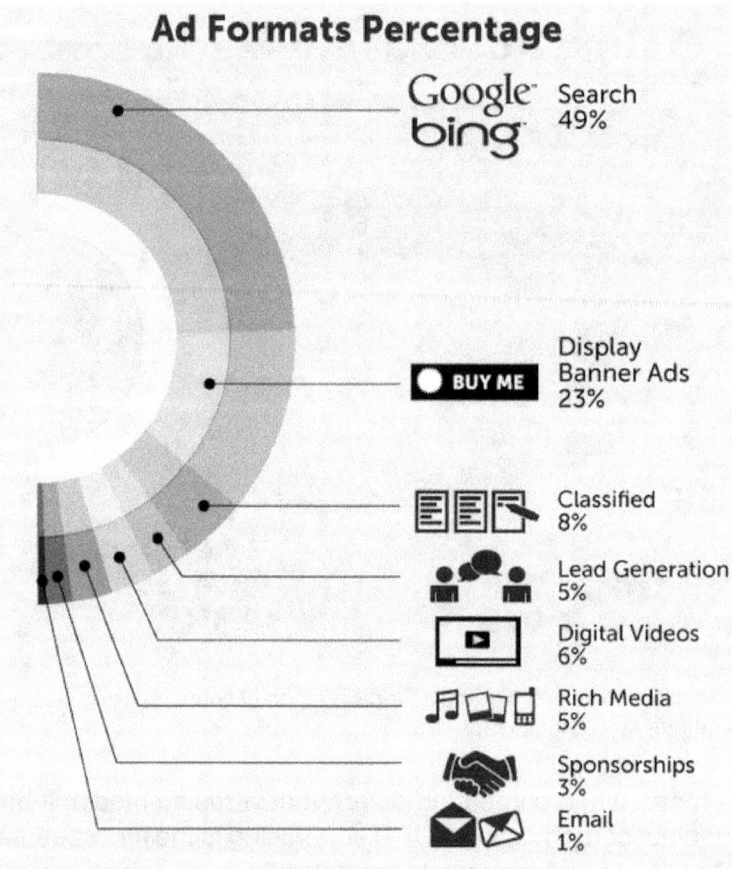

Fig 3.4: Approximately half of online advertisements are Google search engine ads.
Source: http://www.go-gulf.com/

World Search Volumes

In a study conducted by comScore in 2010, it was found that the number of searches made per month topped 13 billion. While the U.S. is the leading country for number of searches performed per month, if you were to add China, Japan, and Korea together, they would surpass that of the U.S. In fact, if you look at Asian search volumes, it becomes clear that it is a region where both Asian and Western businesses can find success penetrating the online markets.

Top 10 Countries by Number of Searches Conducted* December 2009 vs. December 2008 Total Worldwide, Age 15+ - Home & Work Locations Source: comScore qSearch	Searches (MM)		
	Dec-2008	Dec-2009	Percent Change
Worldwide	89,708	131,354	46%
United States	18,688	22,741	22%
China	11,778	13,278	13%
Japan	6,213	9,170	48%
United Kingdom	4,623	6,245	35%
Germany	4,079	5,609	38%
France	3,362	5,425	61%
South Korea	2,796	4,039	44%
Brazil	2,454	3,763	53%
Canada	2,900	3,710	28%
Russian Federation	1,735	3,333	92%

Fig 3.5: Top 10 countries by number of searches performed
Source: http://blog.ineedhits.com/search-news/global-search-volume-us-still-tops-japan-growing-quickly-26237260.html

Google's Worldwide Market Share

If you want to really understand global SEM, you first need to study global search engine market shares. According to a study conducted by Hitwise, in 2011, Google was the most widely used search engine in the world, with a total share of 82%. For some countries, though, Google is not the leader. For example, China's most popular search engine is Baidu, and it increased its share of the total global search engine traffic from 3.3% to 4.9% in two years. This figure is expected to grow as the number of Chinese going online increases, and it will change the picture of the world's search engine market shares.

Search engine ⬥	Market share in May 2011 ⬥	Market share in December 2010[3] ⬥
Google	82.80%	84.65%
Yahoo!	6.42%	6.69%
Baidu	4.89%	3.39%
Bing	3.91%	3.29%
Yandex	1.7%	1.3%
Ask	0.52%	0.56%
AOL	0.3%	0.42%

Fig 3.6: Google possesses over 80% of the World's search engine market share, but due to the increase in the number of Internet users in China, Baidu's share of the overall market is expected to increase.

If you were to exempt China from the list of worldwide search engine market shares, though, Google becomes the favored search engine for most of the countries in the world. Thus, we can say that global SEM essentially is marketing on Google, and that it demands a strong knowledge of how to conduct paid and organic search engine marketing through Google.

Google's Enormous Daily Search Volumes

Looking at official Google data for 2011, there were up to approximately 4,700,000,000 searches performed daily.

Year	Annual Number of Google Searches	Average Searches Per Day
2011	1,722,071,000,000	4,717,000,000
2010	1,324,670,000,000	3,627,000,000
2009	953,700,000,000	2,610,000,000
2008	637,200,000,000	1,745,000,000
2007	438,000,000,000	1,200,000,000
2000	22,000,000,000	60,000,000
1998	3,600,000 *Googles official first year	9,800

Fig 3.7: Searches performed on Google are increasing year by year.
Source: http://www.statisticbrain.com/google-searches/

Country	Search Engines			
	Leader	Share	Runner Up	Share
Argentina	Google	95%	Bing	4%
Australia	Google	87%	Bing	3%
Brazil	Google	97%	Bing	2%
Canada	Google	78%	Bing	6%
Czech Republic	Seznam	45%	Google	45%
China	Baidu	76%	Google	22%
Denmark	Google	97%	Bing	2%
Egypt	Google	95%	Yahoo/Bing	5%
Finland	Google	95%	Other	5%
France	Google	92%	Bing	4%
Germany	Google	89%	t-online	3%
Hong Kong	Yahoo	N/A	Google	N/A
India	Google	95%	Other	5%
Indonesia	Google	92%	Yahoo	5%
Israel	Google	89%	Other	11%
Italy	Google	87%	Virgilio	5%
Japan	Yahoo Japan*	56%	Google	31%
Malaysia	Google	92%	Yahoo	5%
Mexico	Google	91%	Bing	7%
The Netherlands	Google	94%	Vinden	3%
New Zealand	Google	93%	Bing	2%
Philippines	Google	N/A	Yahoo	N/A
Poland	Google	97%	Other	3%
Russia	Yandex	62%	Google	26%
Saudi Arabia	Google	97%	Yahoo/Bing	3%
Slovakia	Google	99%	Yahoo/Bing	1%
South Korea	Naver	73%	Daum	18%
Spain	Google	96%	Yahoo/Bing	4%
Turkey	Google	N/A	Yandex	N/A
United Kingdom / UK	Google	94%	Bing	5%
United States	Google	72%	Yahoo	14%

Fig 3.8: Search engine market shares per country
Source: http://returnonnow.com/2012/06/search-engine-market-share-country/

As noted above, Google controls the major share of the world's search engine market; however, if you dig deeper, the picture becomes more complex. For Asia, in particular, there are search engines other than Google that command a higher share of the market, such as Yahoo! in Japan, Baidu in China, and Naver in Korea. All three of these countries have 2-byte languages. Google, originating in America (with 1-byte English), didn't handle the 2-byte language searches that were required in these Asian countries. It therefore led to other engines capturing more shares of the market early on.

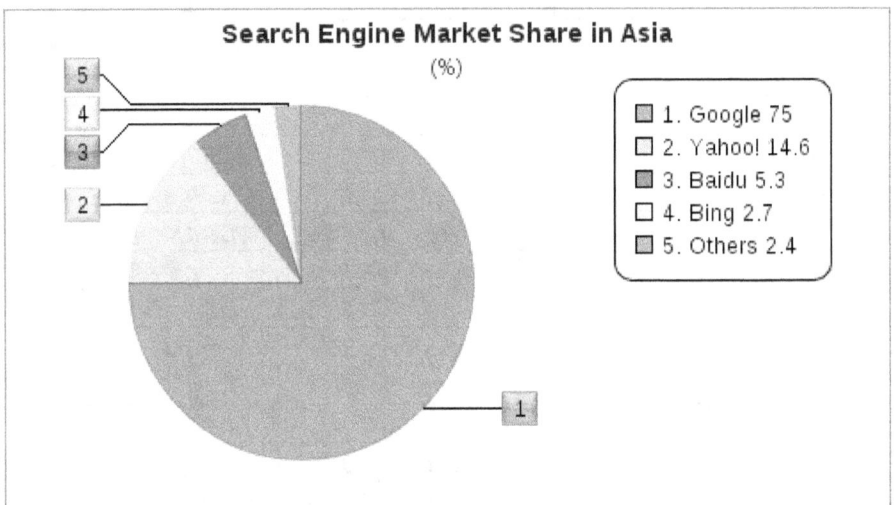

Fig 3.9: Overall search engine shares in Asia
Source: http://www.netmarketshare.com/

Many companies looking to pursue SEM in Asia have had difficulty succeeding because of this significant difference. Indeed, even though Google has the highest overall share of the Asian market in its entirety, businesses penetrating the Asian market with only knowledge of SEM on Google AdWords has led to many exiting in failure. What I always recommend, as the CEO of a global online marketing agency, is to use consulting services or hire your own native speakers when integrating into these Asian markets. For these countries, what is needed are Japanese, Chinese, and Korean professionals who can provide you the marketing, linguistic, cultural, and technical insight needed to be successful.

For those of you who do not have this type of native support, what I have provided in the following chapters is a startup guide to help you in pursuing your global SEM ambitions for the Asian online market. Each chapter will analyze a country or a region in the continent of Asia, providing insight into the respective online markets, all in light of SEM.

The Chinese Online Market

		Reference
Population	1,354,000,000	IMF-World Economic Outlook Database 2012
Internet population	538,000,000	CNNIC 2012
Internet use	39.9%	
Scale of online advertising market	8.11 billion USD	China Internet Watch 2011

- 90% of Chinese Internet users' monthly income is under 5,000 RMB (790 USD) (CNNIC).
- 73.4% of Internet users access the Internet via PC, while 69.3% prefer mobile (CNNIC).
- Approximately 700 million Chinese (52% of the population) will be added to the online community by 2016 (eMarketer).
- In China, approximately 10 million people become part of the online community each month (We Are Social).
- 73.5% of Internet users in China live in metropolitan areas (CNNIC).
- 33.2% of Internet users in China access it at Internet cafes (CNNIC).
- Chinese Internet users spend an average of 18.7 hours online per week (CNNIC).
- 415,000,000 Chinese (77% of the Internet community) chat online (CNNIC).
- 465,000,000 Chinese (86% of the Internet community) watch videos online (China Internet Watch).
- 63% of Internet users play online games (CNNIC).
- Chinese aged 18-27 make up the largest group of Internet users. They spend an average of 5 hours online daily (We Are Social).
- In China, approximately 10,000 searches are performed on search engines every second (We Are Social).

- The search engine marketing industry grew 3 billion USD from 2010 to 2011 (iResearch).
- 61% of online shoppers ask for recommendations from friends or family before they make a purchase.
- In 2011, the value of the Chinese e-commerce market was 1.1 trillion USD (iResearch).
- The results of a survey of the most trustworthy sites in China were (1st) Amazon.cn, (2nd) 360 buy, and (3rd) Tmall (DCCI).
- 319,000,000 Chinese (59% of Internet users) have their own blog (CNNIC).
- Sina Weibo, the largest Chinese social networking service (SNS,) has 300,000,000 users, and 100,000,000 articles are posted online each day (CNNIC).
- Due to Chinese government regulations, Facebook, Twitter, and YouTube are inaccessible in China.

At the end of 2012, the number of Chinese Internet users passed the 538,000,000 mark. However, the percentage of the Chinese population that is on the Internet is still only 39.9%. There is clearly still much room to grow. And, as the Chinese market grows in the future, it will be the largest online market in the world.

Fig 4.1: The Number of Internet users and percentage of Internet use in China
Source: cnnic.net.cn

47

While the number of Asian Internet users is significantly above the number of other regions, this high figure is predominantly attributed to China, which makes up more than half of the total Internet users in Asia.

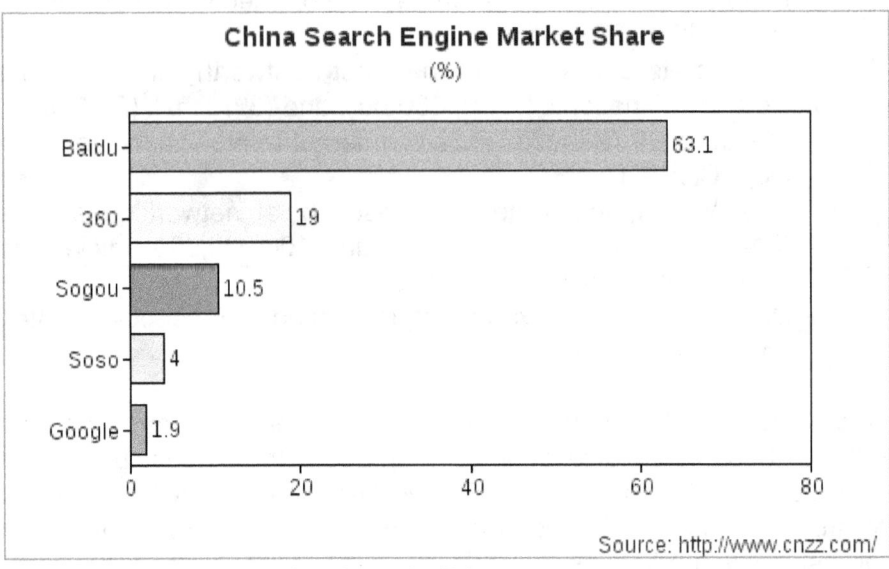

Fig 4.2: Overall search engine shares in China

Currently, more than 78% of Chinese search engine users (approx. 419,000,000 people) turn to Baidu to perform their searches. In China, while word of mouth and promotions via SNS are popular forms of marketing, paid search is just as important. The amount of Chinese searching on Baidu is high, so marketing your business online in China on Baidu is the quickest and most effective way to reach new customers.

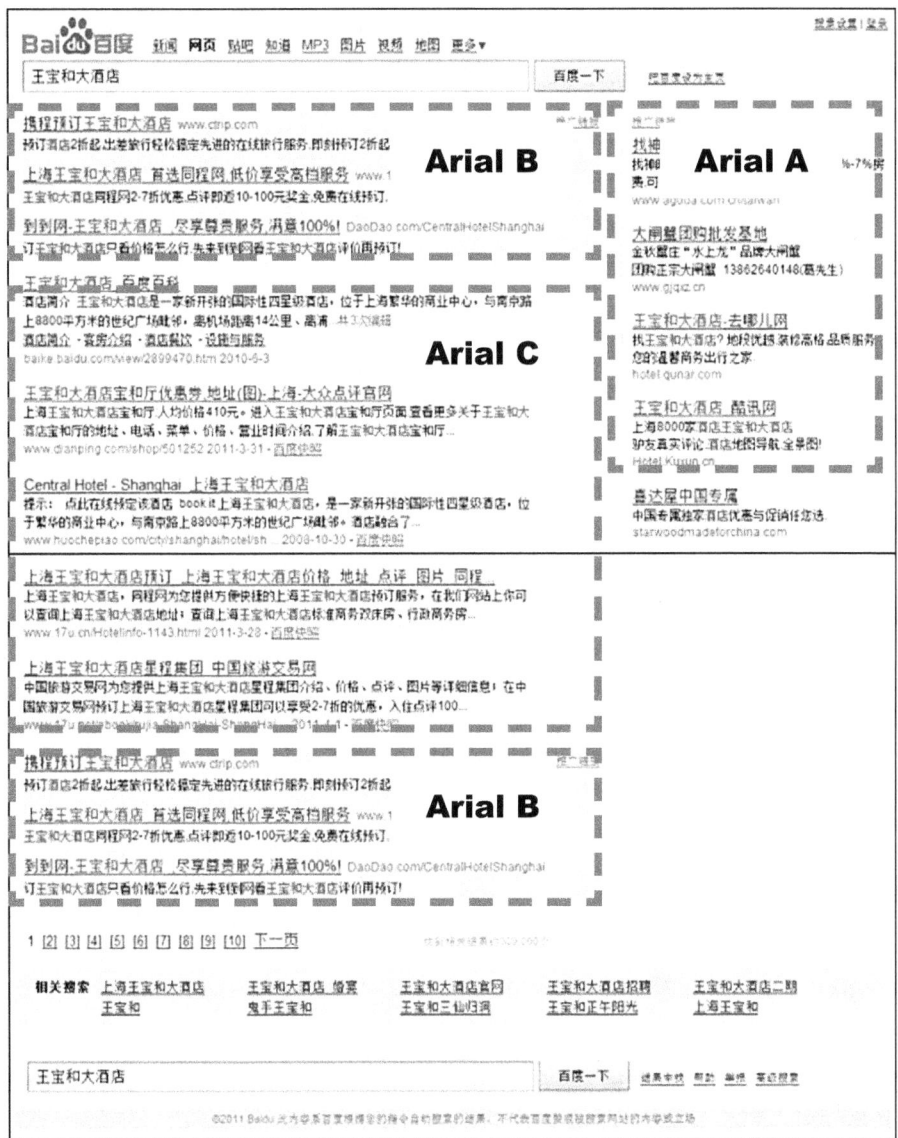

PPC Advertising in China

Baidu's PPC ads are generally displayed in three different ways.

Fig 5.3: The position of an ad will change depending on its performance.

The display order of PPC ads is decided automatically on Baidu. The system measures the relevancy of the searched keyword to an advertiser's registered keyword, the bid price, and the quality score (i.e., ad to landing page relevancy). PPC ads normally appear on the right side -- Area A. If an ad is more relevant to a user's search than average, it can appear in Area B at either the top or bottom. If an ad is deemed to be especially relevant to a search, it can appear in Area C in the middle of the SERP. It's important to check how your ads will appear for the keywords you select.

Keyword Match Type
Baidu features three different keyword match types.

Exact Match – Ads appear for this type when searched keywords exactly match registered keywords and there are no extra words in the query.

Example: When the registered entry is "Japan vacation," ads will appear for: "Japan vacation," but not for "fun Japan vacation," "Japan vacation hotels," "Japan cheap vacation," "vacation Japan," "American vacation," etc.

Phrase Match – Ads appear for this type when at least part of the searched query matches the registered entries or a synonym of the words.

Example: When the registered entry is "Japan vacation," ads will appear for: "Japan vacation," "affordable Japan vacation," "vacation Japan," etc., but not for "Japan travel" or "vacation Tokyo."

Broad Match – Keywords with this match type will bring up ads in the same fashion as Exact and Phrase Match varieties, but also for other related user queries. "Broad Match" means exactly what its name suggests: a broad interpretation of the registered keyword. This entails synonyms and grammatical variations of the keyword.

Example: When the registered keyword entry is "Japan vacation," ads will appear for: "Japan tour," "vacation Tokyo," "Japan hotel," "Japan trip," etc.

Wide Match – Baidu also offers a wider match type for paid search advertisers to take advantage of. It's called "wide match" and it will help advertisers to show ads for keywords with an even more distant relation to their registered entries. Depending on your budget, wide match might not be the best for you though as it can lead to higher advertising costs. Please use it carefully.

Example: When the registered keyword entry is "Japan vacation," ads will appear for: "Tokyo food," "Kyoto souvenirs," etc.

The above four match types should be used accordingly so that your ads will appear or not appear as desired.

Ad Copies

The higher Baidu quality score an ad has, the longer title and description lines it can display. The general format of a text PPC ad on Baidu is a title of up to 14 characters and a description of up to 40 characters. The following image is one of these ads:

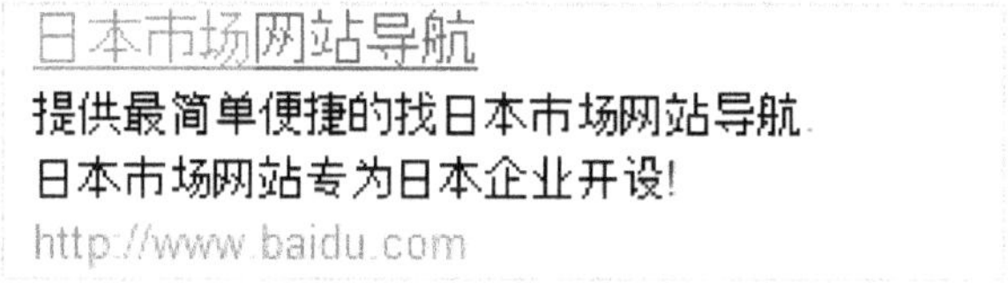

日本市场网站导航
提供最简单便捷的找日本市场网站导航.
日本市场网站专为日本企业开设!
http://www.baidu.com

Fig 4.4: Baidu PPC ad with a short description

Ads with high quality scores, on the other hand, can display titles with up to 25 characters and a description with up to 80 characters. The image below is an extended text ad:

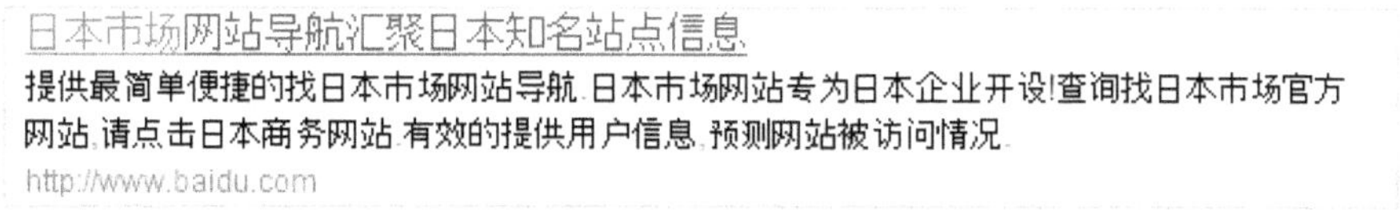

日本市场网站导航汇聚日本知名站点信息.
提供最简单便捷的找日本市场网站导航. 日本市场网站专为日本企业开设!查询找日本市场官方
网站 请点击日本商务网站 有效的提供用户信息. 预测网站被访问情况.
http://www.baidu.com

Fig 4.5: Baidu PPC ad with a long description

This aspect of quality and how it affects ad copy must not be forgotten. It is important that you create lengthier ad copy for the possibility of their appearing in better positions.

Characteristics of Chinese Keywords

One prominent characteristic of Chinese language search queries is that they do not include spaces between words. This is a very important element, and it is recommended that you keep this in mind when creating your keyword list. Consider the following example:

When investigating the monthly search volume for "English language study," (which can be written with or without spaces in Chinese, as many as 5,300 searches were recorded for "英语学习" (no space), but only 50 for "英语 学习" (space present). In English, it is natural to enter spaces between words in a query, but that is not the case for Chinese.

Characteristics of Chinese Ad Copy

Baidu also allows telephone and QQ numbers (QQ is a popular Chinese chat system) to be inserted into PPC ads. Chat is widely used in China for e-commerce customer support, so having a QQ code in your PPC ads is beneficial, because it signals to searchers that you will provide support during the purchase process.

Fig 4.6: It is normal to see phone numbers or QQ codes in Chinese paid search ads.

Baidu Bidding System

Baidu has a bidding system similar to Google AdWords:

- *CRI = bidding price X quality score.*

Baidu's bidding system is based on an index called the Comprehensive Rank Index (CRI). With a high CRI, you can still reach top level display spots even with a bid price lower than competitors. In order to achieve a higher CRI, you must increase your CTR, which can be done by raising the level of your ads' relevancy to users' search queries. In other words, having well written ad copy that creatively integrates keywords being searched will attract more clicks and, thus, increase your CTR. So, even if an advertiser's bid were 2 USD (a price higher than all his competitors), he wouldn't beat out a competitor with a higher CRI and a bid of only 1.80 USD.

Account	Bidding Price	Pricing Mode	Quality Score	CRI	Rank	Click Price
A	2.00	Auto	0.97	1.94	2	1.80
B	1.80	Auto	1.12	2.02	1	1.74
C	1.50	Auto	0.80	1.20	4	1.29
D	1.45	Auto	1.20	1.74	3	1.01
E	1.10	Fixed	0.93	1.02	5	1.10

Fig 4.7: The makeup of how a PPC ad gets its ranking on Baidu.

For Baidu, it is important to remember that a quality score is just as important as bid price. Quality score is measured mainly by the following criteria:

- Keyword compatibility
- Quality of ad copy
- Ad relevance to landing page and keyword
- Having an ICP license
- Load time of the landing page
- Condition of your host server

Regional Settings are Important, Too

For Chinese SEM, it's really important to consider where you want to market within the country before you go about starting your campaigns. China is often thought of as a nation with one people and one language, but in reality, it is much more complex. For example, there are significant differences between the coastal and inland regions in terms of spoken languages, culture, and lifestyle. Not carefully setting the target regions for your campaigns can lead to wasted time and wasted money.

The Baidu Keyword Tool

Baidu has a keyword tool that will provide you with keyword search volume, competition levels for keywords, and peak search periods (i.e., which month a keyword is searched most). This tool can be accessed via the following link:

- http://u.baidu.com/?module=default&controller=Reg&action=-regUser&appid=3 (registration required)

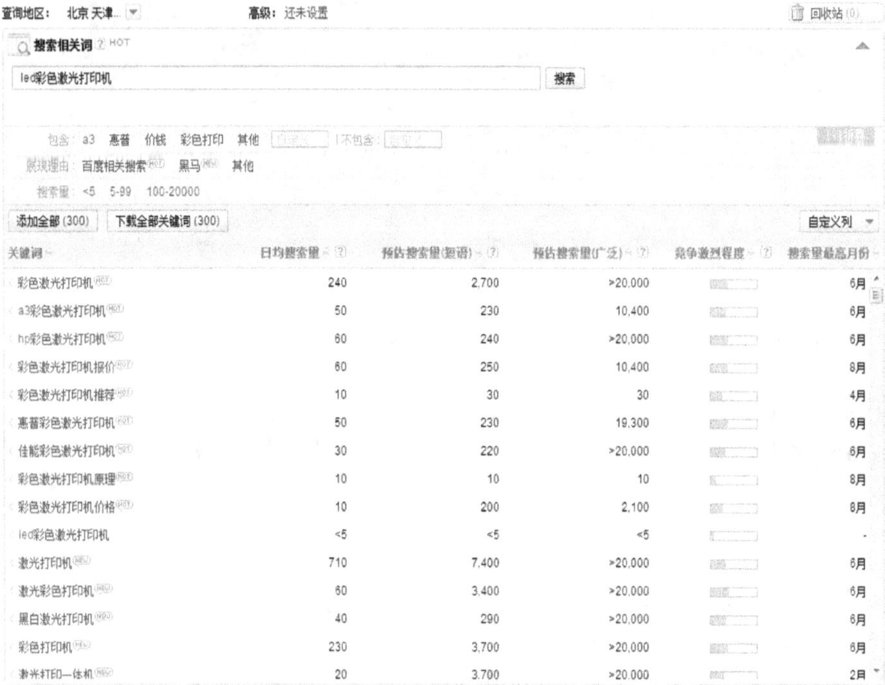

关键词	日均搜索量	预估搜索量(短语)	预估搜索量(广泛)	竞争激烈程度	搜索量最高月份
彩色激光打印机	240	2,700	>20,000		6月
a3彩色激光打印机	50	230	10,400		6月
hp彩色激光打印机	60	240	>20,000		6月
彩色激光打印机报价	60	250	10,400		8月
彩色激光打印机推荐	10	30	30		4月
惠普彩色激光打印机	50	230	19,300		6月
佳能彩色激光打印机	30	220	>20,000		6月
彩色激光打印机原理	10	10	10		8月
彩色激光打印机价格	10	200	2,100		8月
led彩色激光打印机	<5	<5	<5		-
激光打印机	710	7,400	>20,000		6月
激光彩色打印机	60	3,400	>20,000		6月
黑白激光打印机	40	290	>20,000		6月
彩色打印机	230	3,700	>20,000		6月
激光打印一体机	20	3,700	>20,000		2月

Fig 4.8: Baidu's keyword tool

In order to use the Baidu Keyword Tool, you'll need to first create a paid search account with them. Only then can you access all the valuable data that will assist you in planning for your Chinese SEM.

Baidu Trends

Baidu has a tool that is very similar to Google Trends. Unlike Google's version, however, which provides numerical data gathered from user searches all over the world, Baidu only provides information related to China (as you would expect). One other major difference between the two, though, is that explicit figures are not shown on Baidu's version; rather, data collected by Baidu is used to show which keywords are trending at specific periods of time. By using Baidu's tool to organize your SEM, you can estimate when more traffic will come to your site. Furthermore, this tool provides other useful information such as alternative keywords with a high level of relevancy to yours, search data associated with users' gender, data regarding users' educational background, and even regional statistics.

 ◆ Baidu Trends: http://index.baidu.com/

Chinese SEO

Until 2009, most of Baidu's first SERP was filled with paid search ads, so even if you were to attempt SEO, reaching the first page was more dream than reality. Since 2009, however, Baidu has shifted its engine to operating on the Phoenix Nest Platform, which essentially gave its SERPs more of a Google-like feel (i.e., balance between paid and organic results).

The Title Tag is Key

Title tags are very important on Baidu. It is crucial that target keywords are present and integrated into the title tag. Also, for Baidu it seems that keywords inserted closer to the beginning of the tag are more influential. You do not want to insert more than two keywords, though. The length of a Baidu title tag should ideally be 30 characters or fewer. Overall, since title tags take center stage in the SERPs, it is important that you create them with the purpose of attracting clicks. This can be done by inserting the keywords that users are looking for into the title tag.

 ◆ Example of a Chinese title tag:
   <title>让日本的旅游成为您最好的回忆！日本旅游请到ABC旅行社</title>

 ◆ English translation:
   <title>A trip to Japan you'll remember! For Japanese vacations, see ABC Travel.<title>

Copywriting for Meta Tags is Effective

Currently, Google does not consider meta data that important for its ranking of search results; Baidu, on the other hand, does. Since your site's meta descriptions will be shown in search results, it is highly recommended you write them accurately and persuasively, in addition to including target keywords. This should lead to more clicks. The length of the meta description should ideally be 75 to 150 characters.

- Chinese meta tag examples:
  <meta name="keywords" content="日本, 旅游, 观光情报,旅游团,自由行,旅游,ABC旅行社"/>

  <meta name="description" content="日本旅游的观光情报和购物情报的综合旅游网页，为了让您的日本旅游成为您最好的回忆，我们向顾客提供各种旅游团和自由行的情报，日本旅游请到ABC旅行社。"/>

- English translations:
  <meta name="keywords" content=" Japan, travel, tourism information, tours, vacation, travel, ABC Travel "/>

  <meta name="description" content="Our site contains various information on traveling and shopping in Japan. ABC Travel provides tours and individual travel plans that have been developed to meet the needs and wants of our customers. For your trip to Japan, contact ABC Travel."/>

Save the Best for the Top

For your website's SEO, putting more important text at the top of each target page is important, because it has been found that Baidu values this area more in its algorithms. Make sure to exercise caution with your content, though, as Baidu does penalize for keyword stuffing.

Baidu Favors Websites with Volume

It has been found that Baidu ranks sites with a higher volume of textual content better than their lower volume counterparts. This content cannot be just any content, though. It must be rich content, not just filler. Always create content that keeps the website viewers' interests in mind.

Backlinks are Important to Baidu

Baidu, like Google, places a significant amount of value on the number of quality backlinks a site has. The backlinks for your site need to be from sites that are related to your own, so a large amount of links from just any site will not do. Recklessly building a link portfolio from irrelevant, low quality sites will lead to a decrease in your site's ranking, and, if the situation becomes too spammy, you could be removed from Baidu SERPs. Link building on Baidu is not as risky as it is on Google, though, so if you do plan on buying some, just make sure they are top-notch quality.

Hosting Issue

In order to perform SEO on Baidu, it is recommended you host your site in China. The Chinese government has established a conservative firewall, termed "The Great Firewall of China," which can prevent overseas sites from being accessed domestically. The mere existence of this system essentially slows down foreign sites' load times, because they have to pass through it every time a Chinese user attempts to gain access. If you are planning to perform SEO on your site and it is hosted outside of China, make sure to first check the load time; your SEO strategies could end up being futile if Baidu is unable to effectively crawl your site. Even for paid search on Baidu, your site's load time will be taken into consideration. In order to check your website's load time, use Baidu Analytics.

If you are planning to host your site in China, you will first need to obtain an Internet Content Provider (ICP) license. This license is only available to companies founded in China or with subsidiaries based there. If you don't have this, though, hosting through a company in Hong Kong or Singapore can help with site speed issues that will arise.

Baidu Webmaster Tools

Google's Webmaster Tools (http://www.google.com/webmasters/tools/) is a widely used program that can provide you various data on your website, but Baidu also has its own version: http://zhanzhang.baidu.com/.You can find out how to use the Baidu tool on this page:

- http://zhanzhang.baidu.com/welcome

Although the page is in Chinese, it can be translated into a language of your liking if you use a browser that has a translation function, such as Google Chrome.

Through Baidu's Webmaster Tools, you will be able to register your website's site map. By registering your site map beforehand, you can avoid Baidu crawling errors and know which pages in your site aren't being indexed properly. Registering your site map will not, however, guarantee your ranking will increase in the SERPs.

Registering URLs

The following link is to Baidu's indexation application page:

- http://zhanzhang.baidu.com/sitesubmit

While applying for your site's indexation does not guarantee it will be indexed, there is the possibility that you can increase the speed of the whole process, so it is highly recommended.

Baidu Traffic Analysis Tool
Baidu provides a free tool called Baidu Analytics, which provides traffic data for your website:

- http://tongji.baidu.com/web/welcome/login

What is nice about this tool is that it not only provides website traffic data, it also has data that can be used for your SEO.

The features of Baidu Analytics that can be used for your site's SEO analysis:

Item	Description
SEO Analysis	The maximum score for the SEO analysis is 100 points. High scores signify proper SEO, and low scores, a need for improvement. Receiving a 100 point score does not ensure a high ranking on Baidu, but the analysis data is generally a good reference.
Ranking Inquiry	Up to ten keywords' ranking data can be taken.
Indexation Inquiry	This tool shows you how many of your pages are actually indexed on Baidu. If the number of pages in your website is below the number of pages shown in the inquiry, there was a problem that occurred during the crawling of your site.
Load Time Evaluation	This tool measures the load time of your site. If load times are significantly slow for your site, it is not only bad for your SEO, it's not ideal for your site's viewers either. Changing hosts or fixing your pages to speed up the times is highly recommended.
Link Analysis	The Link Analysis tool allows you to see what sites are linking to yours. By knowing what types of sites are linked to yours, you will know what is needed to increase your site's ranking. Generally speaking, you want to have a large number of trustworthy sites as your backlinks.

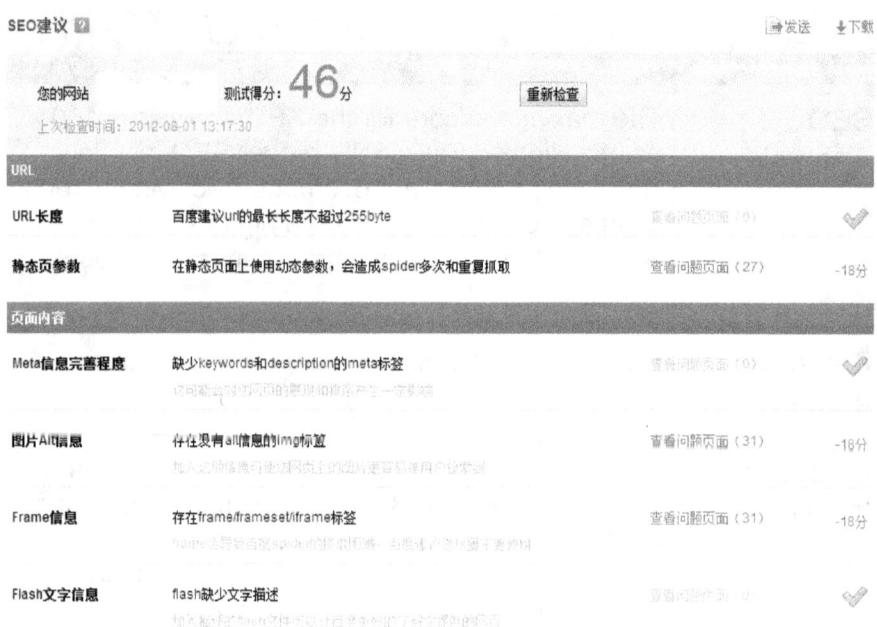

Fig 4.9: A screenshot of Baidu's SEO analytics tool, wherein you can find out a website's SEO score.

After inserting Baidu Analytics' traffic access tags into your site's source code and pushing the SEO scan button, Baidu will perform an SEO evaluation of your website. This scan will point out the problematic areas of your site, such as any lengthy URLs, meta tag settings, and Frame or Flash use. Ultimately, it will provide you a comprehensive score.

Search Engine Directories in China

In China, there are a number of directories on which you can register your site for SEO purposes. When performing SEO in China, you should definitely consider registering your site on the following directories:

- http://www.2345.com/
  Registration URL: http://bbs.2345.com/forumdisplay.
  php?fid=27&page=1&filter=type&typeid=9

- http://123.sogou.com/
  Registration URL: http://123.sogou.com/about/shoulu.html

- http://hao.360.cn/
  Registration URL: http://hao.360.cn/url.html

More Information about China

In China, there is a government operated firewall that blocks a significant amount of foreign sites, to the point that it has been given the name "The Great Firewall of China." If you are trying to promote your site in China and it isn't passing through The Great Firewall, then Chinese internet users will be unable to access your site. In order to check if your site is able to be accessed by Chinese internet users, please visit the following site:

Fig 4.10: Greatfirewallofchina.org, a website that allows you to check if your site is able to be accessed by domestic Chinese internet users

It is very easy to use this site: All you have to do is enter your site's URL and press "test." The page that follows will inform you whether or not your site can be accessed in China.

When a site is accessible in China, the following screen with green "OKs" will appear.

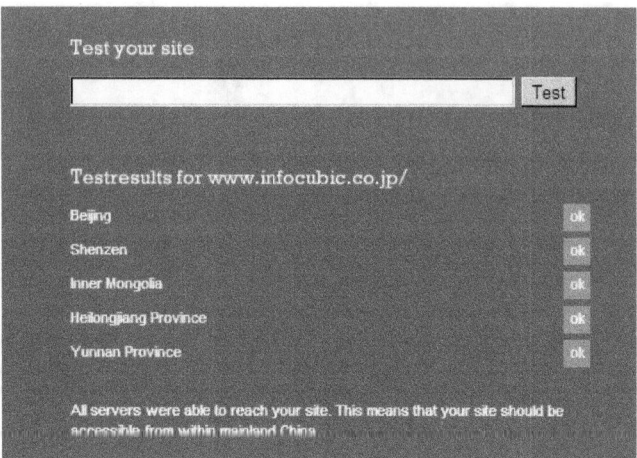

Fig 4.11: The green lights indicate that a site is viewable in China.

Some sites, such as www.youtube.com, are not accessible. This is designated by red "FAIL" symbols. The Facebook and Twitter site is also inaccessible.

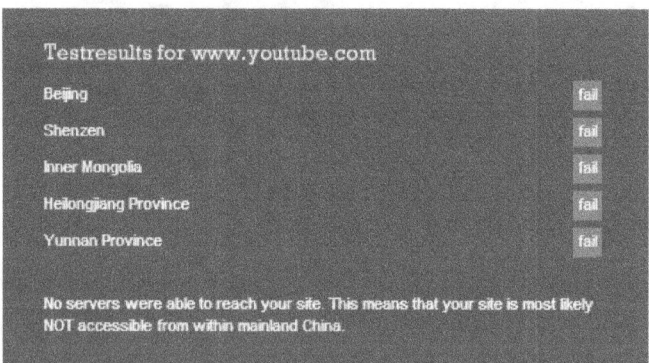

Fig 4.12: The red lights indicate that a site is not viewable in China.

If you enter your site's URL and the red "FAIL" symbols appear, there is the chance that the content in your site breaches China's Internet regulations. All that can be done to fix this problem is for you to change the content of your site.

The Japanese Online Market

		Reference
Population	127,611,000	IMF-World Economic Outlook Database 2012
Internet population	100,457,000	World Bank 2012
Internet use	79.1%	
Scale of online advertising market	618,900,000,000 JPY	Dentsu 2011

Japan is one of the countries in the world with the highest rate of Internet use; for Asia, Japan only falls behind South Korea. The size of the Japanese market is quite large, so it is an exceptionally attractive market for Western companies looking to penetrate the Asian online market.

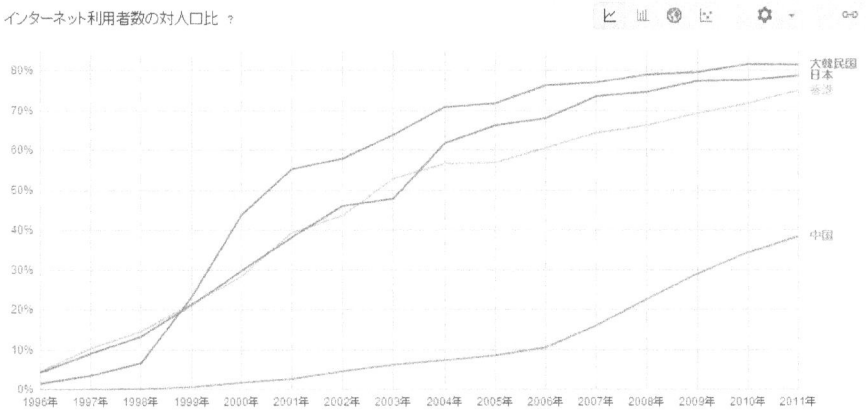

Key: Korea (red), Japan (blue), Hong Kong (orange) & China (green)

Fig 5.1: For Asia, Japan is only behind South Korea in total Internet use per country.

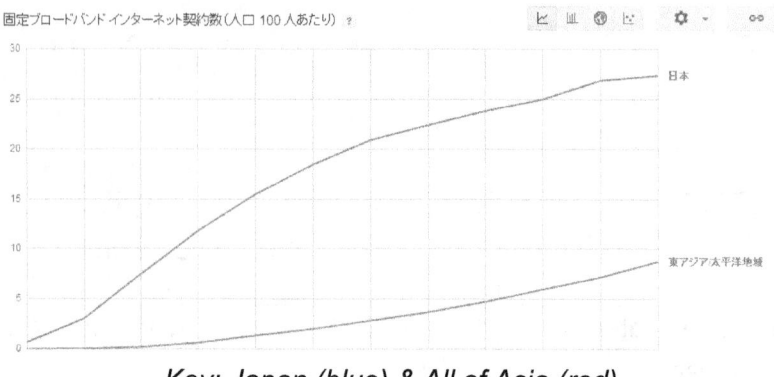

Key: Japan (blue) & All of Asia (red)

Fig 5.2: Japan is also a leading Asian country for broadband internet use. It is exceptionally higher than the Asian average.

In light of the data above, it can be said with confidence that Japan is a country with a developed online market. It isn't like other developed markets around the world, though, not even other Asian countries. Just like the Japanese offline market, the online market also has a unique composition when compared to similar-sized markets of the West. These traits are important to keep in mind when you are planning Internet marketing strategies for Japan. In this chapter, I will touch on a few of these items.

The Japanese Search Engine Market

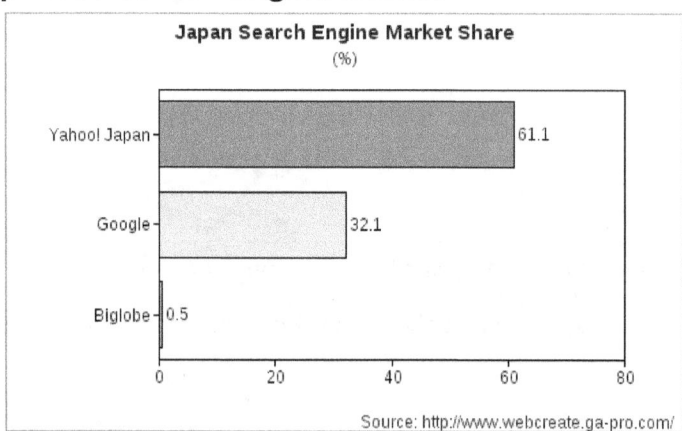

Fig 5.3: Overall search engine shares in Japan

The leading search engine in Japan in terms of overall market share is Yahoo! Japan. Google comes in a strong second, though, and it continues to get more popular. What's interesting to note, however, is that currently Yahoo! Japan is using Google's search engine to operate its searches. Therefore, Yahoo!'s share of the search engine market in Japan can actually be attributed to Google. If you were to calculate the search engine share by search engine algorithm use, 90% of the overall share would belong to Google.

PPC Advertising in Japan

Yahoo! Japan and Google are the two most used search engines in Japan. I therefore recommend advertising on both. In the past, both search engines had their own PPC platform on which advertisers would run their campaigns. Now, however, Yahoo! Japan's PPC advertising platform, Promotional Ads, uses the same engine as Google AdWords. This makes the transition of running campaigns on Promotional Ads smoother for the AdWords veteran. But, it must be said that both platforms are not identical, and so it can take some time to master Promotional Ads. Simply taking your campaign data on AdWords and transferring it to Promotional Ads is not possible. Certain modifications must be made. Promotional Ads differs from other countries' Yahoo! paid search advertising services, as well. It is essentially a Japanese service, so if a user were to set up an account on Promotional Ads, he could not use it to advertise on Yahoo! in other countries. Other countries' Yahoo! search engines are using the Bing platform anyway. Also, signing up for their advertising service requires Japanese language skills, so this is also something that must be considered. In this section, I will focus on Yahoo! Japan's Promotional Ads service and its many features that differ from Google's AdWords. It is my hope to help you adequately prepare yourself for paid search advertising in Japan on Yahoo! *and* Google AdWords.

Promotional Ads: Unique Features

The Yahoo! Japan PPC platform has many features that are similar to AdWords, so overall it will be fairly easy for AdWords advertisers to run paid search campaigns once they have become accustomed to its format. However, there are certain differences that might force users to spend a little more time than usual for their daily operations.

First and foremost, most of the PPC platform is available in English. The only problematic areas for non-Japanese speakers will be the display network and certain features such as the help center and agency portal, as these have not all been localized for the English language market. Linguistics aside, though, there are other certain aspects of Promotional Ads that might pose a bit of a challenge for those unfamiliar with the platform. I would like to introduce a few in particular: (1) campaign, ad group, and ad and keyword limits; (2) the data import feature; and (3) campaign/ad group/keyword settings. Understanding the differences between Promotional Ads and AdWords with respect to these areas will definitely help to smooth your ad campaign operations.

1. Data Limitations

Below is a list of the limitations for Promotional Ads. For the purpose of comparison, I have also included AdWords' limits. As you will see, Yahoo! Japan does not allow the volume that Google does. Many will argue, though, that it provides enough.

Item	Promotional Ads Limit	AdWords Limit
Campaigns	100 per account	10,000 per account
Ad groups	2,000 per campaign	20,000 per campaign
Ads	50 per ad group	50 per ad group
Keywords	2,000 keywords per ad group 5,000 keywords per campaign 50,000 keywords per account	20,000 per ad group 5,000,000 per account

For those who find the Promotional Ads limits disappointing, there is still at least one solution. If you were to advertise through a Japanese SEM agency, it is possible to contact Yahoo! Japan and have certain limitations increased. This is a feature only available for SEM agencies though.

2. Data import feature
The Promotional Ads platform facilitates the process of importing and editing large amounts of data with its import feature. Rather than using an editor program such as that which AdWords provides, Promotional Ads accepts a bulk .csv file as a medium for importing all the data necessary for running an account. This is not a problem for people with plenty of Excel experience; however, for those who do not have a strong command of the Excel program, this feature of Yahoo! can be quite troublesome. The larger a Promotional Ads account is, the bigger the files will be and the longer they will take to upload. Also, it is important to note that one mistake will cause the import of your data to fail. This can frustrate even the seasoned professional, as it wastes a lot of time. So, it is always important that you set more time aside for your account operations on Promotional Ads.

Why doesn't Yahoo! Japan offer an editor you ask? Well, Yahoo! Japan does have one, but it doesn't operate in the same fashion as Google's—this will be elaborated upon later. So, advertisers are left to import their data via .csv files with rows upon rows of data. Make sure your Excel skills are up to par and you enter all the data necessary before attempting to import on Yahoo! Japan.

3. Campaign/ad group/keyword settings
The campaign, ad group, and keyword level settings available on Yahoo! are all available on AdWords, so if you're an AdWords professional, you don't have to stress over learning how to operate new features. Fortunately, for your campaign settings, most of the features that AdWords includes are also available on Promotional Ads. However, certain advanced options are limited or non-existent. For reference, I have listed some features below that are <u>not featured</u> on Promotional Ads. Some of these—or even all of these—are used regularly by AdWords marketers, so knowing beforehand the alternative measures you will have to take in order to get around the lack of options will help you to run your paid search campaigns more smoothly:

- IP exclusion
  If you would like to exclude a specific IP address from being able to see your ads, this is the feature to use. This is often used to prevent being charged for clicking your own ads.

- Keyword matching options
  This feature allows you to select whether you want ads showing for plurals, misspelling or other similar alternatives to your registered keywords.

- Automatic conversion-based bidding strategy
  Advertisers who would like to have Yahoo! automatically bid according to their conversion data (like this AdWords feature allows) will unfortunately not be able to find it.

- Campaign/ad group/keyword level automated rule creation
  This is another feature of AdWords that you will not find on Promotional Ads. You will have to stick to manual operations when managing your account.

Promotional Ads: Text Ad Characteristics

One aspect of Promotional Ads that many advertisers like is the additional space they are provided to compose their ad copy. I have included a chart that compares AdWords and Promotional Ads' character limits for 2-byte Japanese text ads.

Item	Promotional Ads	AdWords
Title	15 characters	12 characters
Description 1	19 characters	17 characters
Description 2	19 characters	17 characters
Display URL	29 characters	17 characters

What's more, in addition to the extra characters advertisers are provided, there is also a wider range of characters that users can incorporate into their ads on Yahoo!'s service. I have provided some of the characters that Google does not allow to be used in AdWords, but which can be inserted into text ads run on Promotional Ads.

Character Type	Example
Underbar	＿
Three dot leader	…
Operators	= ≠ ∞
Arrows	⇒ ⇔ → ← ↑ ↓
Other symbols	￥ ＃ ♪ @ 〆 ※ 〒 ★ ☆

Reference: Yahoo Promotional Ads

The extra number and types of characters that can be utilized through Yahoo! Japan's Promotional Ads is one of the attractive characteristics of the Japanese paid search platform. The higher level of freedom in copywriting that the medium provides advertisers can lead to higher CTRs for your ads. I recommend using the extra features that Yahoo! provides so that you may experience higher CTRs for your ads and, hopefully, more overall sales of your products/services.

The YDN

To expand advertisers' reach even further, Yahoo! Japan also features a display advertising service, the Yahoo! Display Ad Network (YDN). The YDN is in many ways similar to Google's Display Network (GDN). What it does is essentially make banner advertising possible on various types of websites for users located across Japan. It also includes various targeting features that help to narrow the scope of advertising campaigns so the best traffic possible is gained. This means that users are capable of advertising to a select group of Internet users in a small Japanese city or millions of Japanese throughout the nation. Nearly all of the targeting capabilities that AdWords features, such as ad time scheduling, website exclusion, selection of target users' gender or age group, and others, are included in the YDN.

Advertisers used to the GDN might find the system a bit challenging, though, as not all data or targeting options that AdWords' version provides are available on the YDN; the overall format is different, too.

One of the biggest challenges, though, is that it is only provided in Japanese. This, along with the other items listed above, are some things that must be taken into account before attempting any display ad campaigns. Nonetheless, the YDN is a relatively advanced display advertising platform and can provide effective targeting of your advertisements in Japan. I have chosen the following screenshots to illustrate the process of organizing a display campaign on the YDN.

When structuring your campaign, there are various targeting settings, one of which labeled "interest categories". This setting allows you to target the interests of Yahoo users. A wide range of topics is available to choose from, such as car tires, social issues, or flower viewing.

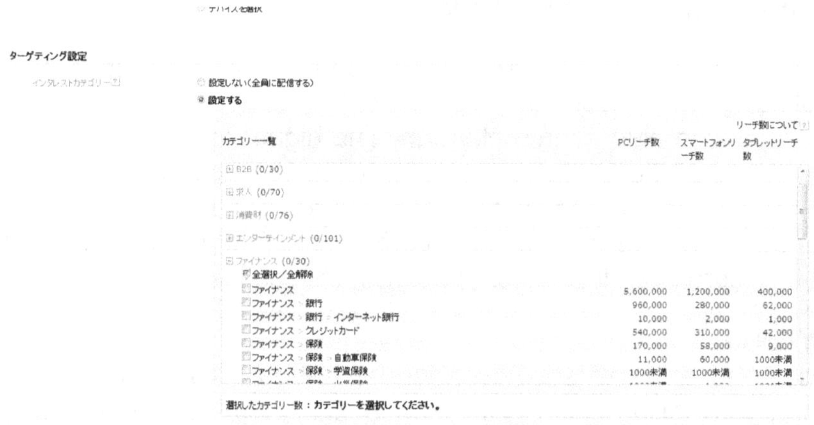

Fig 5.4: Screenshot of the "Interest Categories" target setting

There are also website categories, which allow you to narrow the types of sites on which you would like to run your campaigns. Here too, categories are numerous. Some of the top level website categories include news, SNS, entertainment and specialty sites.

Getting more granular, the YDN also includes an age targeting setting, which actually has a more defined list of age groups than the GDN. There are even age groups that include minors.

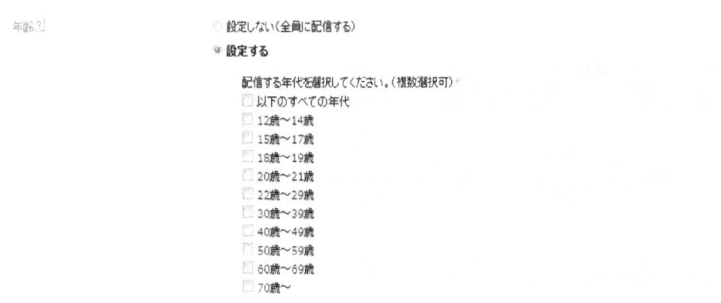

Fig 5.6: Screenshot of the age group target setting

Another important targeting setting is the regional targeting feature. Like the GDN, various local targeting can be done through regional settings. This allows for more effective targeting and can consequently lower CPAs. If you want to ensure a more effective campaign from the start, definitely utilize this setting.

Although the YDN is lacking in some minute features when compared to the GDN, in areas such as keyword targeting or the number of banner sizes that can be advertised, it serves as a fairly complex and effective display advertising platform. It can even be argued that you can perform more effective targeting on Yahoo! Japan, because websites and user interests have been categorized specifically for the Japanese market. Some advertisers actually have seen better results on the YDN when running campaigns simultaneously on the GDN. This goes to show that for Japanese display advertising, Yahoo! Japan should not be disregarded as one of your key media. I recommend checking out the YDN and testing its effectiveness yourself.

Promotional Ads: Useful Tools
Yahoo! Japan Promotional Ads' tools are not as advanced as AdWords' overall, but they have most of the same features and even have some that AdWords doesn't, so they are useful for planning and optimizing your Japanese SEM campaigns on Yahoo!. In this section, I will introduce two tools in particular that are undoubtedly beneficial when running paid search campaigns.

The Yahoo! Keyword Advice Tool

The keyword research tool that Promotional Ads provides its clients is in many ways similar to that of AdWords. You won't find as many keywords provided to you as you will on Google's Keyword Planner, but the data provided through the tool is in many ways much more thorough. For example, just putting in the URL of the site you want to advertise will give you a list of up to hundreds of keywords with the following information:

- ◆ Competitiveness
- ◆ Monthly Search Volume
- ◆ Estimated Average CPC
- ◆ Estimated Average Position
- ◆ Estimated CTR
- ◆ Estimated Impressions / Day
- ◆ Estimated Clicks / Day
- ◆ Estimated Cost / Day

The above items are provided individually for PC/tablets, mobiles, and smartphones, so you can see right away how keywords should be bid according to device.

Some other great features of the Yahoo! Japan Keyword Advice Tool are the changes in search volume graph and demographic data that are accessible via the same page. With the search volume changes graph, you can view how often your group of keywords was searched over the last year in both monthly and hourly increments. This type of data can help you adjust your bidding and overall advertising strategy for your campaigns. The other feature, demographic data, is valuable, because it shows you the locations, days of the week, and the genders and age ranges of users searching for the keyword group you designate. All of this data is available through Promotional Ads' Keyword Advice Tool. Some might feel the data provided is much more than what is actually needed to run a successful campaign, but for individuals who are looking for the most thorough keyword data they can find, Yahoo! Japan does a pretty good job.

The Yahoo! Japan Tag Manager

Another great tool that can really make tracking your online marketing performance hassle-free is the Yahoo! Japan Tag Manager. The Tag Manager is a convenient program that allows users to analyze multiple types of tracking data using only one universal tag. What this means is the Tag Manager program can be your one-stop solution to tracking the performance of your Japanese SEM campaigns, because both Promotional Ads and AdWords data can be tracked using the platform. Of course, if you want to track data from sources other than Yahoo! and Google (e.g. Criteo, Adobe SiteCatalyst, or MicroAd BLADE), that is possible as well. Below I have listed some of the great features of the Tag Manager for your reference:

Some of the numerous benefits of using the Tag Manager are:

- The analysis of your overall performance is simplified.
- More than 100 different types of tags are supported.
- Time and labor inserting a variety of media's tags is reduced.
- Web page load time can be reduced.
- Tag errors are identified in real time.
- Tags can be turned on and off in real time.
- Data loss can be prevented.

As you can see, the Yahoo! Japan Tag Manager is a convenient tool that includes many great features that facilitate the process of performance assessment. It is also easily accessible via the "support tools" tab on the Promotional Ads management screen. For more detailed information regarding the Tag Manager, visit the official site at: http://tagmanager.yahoo.co.jp/ (in Japanese).

Japanese SEO

In 2010, Yahoo! Japan announced it would start running its searches using Google's search algorithms. Up until the change, it was necessary to perform SEO in light of both search engines. Now that both services use the same search engine, SEO has become easier in many respects; now, measures only need to be based off Google's algorithms. Thus, rankings are nearly always the same for both search engines. Speaking of other search engines, there is Bing in Japan, which comes in third place behind Yahoo! Japan and Google; however, its share of the market is very low, and companies rarely optimize their sites to it.

Japan's SEO market has changed significantly within the last few years. The old standard SEO strategy of general and pay-per-performance link building is now shifting to a focus on strengthening website content and link earning, mirroring industry developments happening in the West. This is due to the strong actions Google has taken in recent years to eliminate search engine spam. In light of this, Japanese companies, just like their Western counterparts, will need to decide which path they want to take regarding their site's SEO. Depending on whether they approach SEO as a short-or long-term method of increasing their site's traffic, the measures to be implemented will differ. SEO isn't merely a process to improve a site's search engine ranking; it is, instead, defined as a way to improve one's site traffic organically with respect to the goals of your business. To predict the future of Japanese SEO, I would say all one needs to do is analyze what measures companies in the West are implementing into their own sites. It's only a matter of time until it fully makes its way to Japan.

Google and Yahoo! Japan: SERP Differences

As stated above, Yahoo! Japan uses the same algorithms as Google for its search engine, so the organic search rankings are the same; however, there are differences in the way the organic and paid search results appear visually.

For paid search results, for example, Google includes three that appear at the top of the page with a salmon-colored background. Yahoo!, on the other hand, has up to five and the background is white, just like the organic results. Consequently, Ads on Yahoo! are not as apparent as on Google and could lead to higher CTRs. Also, if an ad appears in this top area, it will also appear at the bottom of the search results page, which is another feature different from Google.

Fig 5.7: The number of ads at the top of Google and Yahoo! Japan's SERP is different. Here Yahoo is presenting 5 for the Japanese keyword "insurance".

Other major differences between the two search engines include related search terms, shopping results, and the map feature. For related search results, while Yahoo! Japan includes them at the top and bottom of the SERP, Google only lists the entries at the bottom.

Fig 5.8: Yahoo! Japan also includes related searches in the top area of the SERP.

The map feature of Yahoo! Japan uses the same engine as Google's, so it's identical in that respect, but Yahoo! Japan has its own local business posting service called Yahoo! Loco. This service shows business listings utilizing the Yahoo! Japan map feature. In order to take advantage of this service, you are required to register your business on Yahoo Loco: http://loco.yahoo.co.jp/).

Fig 5.9: Screenshot of Yahoo! Loco

It is in this fashion that Yahoo! Japan's and Google's SERPs differ. Knowing how they contrast is certainly something to always keep in mind, so that you can manage your Japanese SEO in a more effective manner.

Naver Matome and SEO

Naver Matome (http://matome.naver.jp/) is great content curation site that has recently become quite popular in Japan. Although Naver is a Korean company, the site Matome is purely Japanese: the Japanese subsidiary of Naver, LINE, created and maintains the site. Naver Matome is free to register on and allows its users to create curations of the content that they find interesting on the Web. Titles, body text, links, pictures, and more can all be collaged together to create their own blog-like page.

What's exciting about Naver Matome in terms of SEO, is that in early 2013, Yahoo! Japan signed a deal with Naver to include Matome posts on the first page of Yahoo! Japan's SERPs. The SEO implications of this are that, essentially, with enough practice, curations could be used as a means of achieving higher rank on Yahoo! Japan's search results. As signing up for an account is free, in the years to come, there could be an influx of SEOs all trying to tap into the resources that Matome provides. As it is a free service, there is nothing to lose by creating an account. So, I recommend trying some curating for yourself to see if you can create a post that will rank for your target keywords.

Search Engine Directories in Japan

For Japanese SEO, there are also various high quality directories you can take advantage of. The majority of them charge a fee to register, but they are definitely worth considering. When just starting out in the Japanese online market, it is recommended that you register your new site on at least one of these directories:

- http://business.yahoo.co.jp/bizx/
- http://www.emachi.co.jp/
- http://www.xlisting.co.jp/Service/Xrecommend/index.html
- http://www.jlisting.jp/jdirectory/

More Information about Japan

Japan, like other Asian countries, has its own unique array of social media platforms. While social media isn't purely SEM, it can play an important role overall in an online marketing campaign. Indeed, there is often synergy that forms between SEM and social media marketing regardless of the country in which you are advertising. In this section, I will discuss elements of Japan's social media market.

When looking at the SNS market share spread for Japan, surprisingly, Facebook doesn't come in first. The top share of the SNS market belongs to one of the original Japanese social networking services, mixi. Data released for 2013 indicates there were approximately 27.1 million registered users on mixi. On the other hand, the total number of Facebook users was measured at 19.6 million.

Even so, Japan's social media market is not that large when compared to the West. Since the total number of Internet users in Japan amounts to 100 million, less than 30% are on mixi and even fewer on Facebook. Other popular Western SNS, such as LinkedIn, with 9.7 million registered users, also have a presence in Japan, but are even less noticeable than Facebook So, as you can see, there is still much room to grow in Japan. This doesn't mean that digital marketers should avoid integrating social media into their online marketing strategies. What is important is knowing the differences between popular SNS in Japan and those in the West. Here, I will introduce some of the key differences between Facebook and mixi, so that you can figure out which medium would be best for you to utilize in your Japanese online marketing campaigns.

Account Creation
For mixi accounts, in order to register, you need to enter a valid Japanese cell phone number. Facebook, on the other hand, doesn't require this to create an account. This is a big difference that can impede foreign marketers from using mixi's services.

User Names and Photos
Another significant difference between the two SNS is the registered user names and photos you will find. On the Japanese native SNS, mixi, you will find that most users have registered a pen name for themselves and haven't uploaded any personal photos. This is largely due to the level in which privacy is valued in Japan. Japanese Facebook users, on the other hand, are more willing to post their real name and personal photos, because it is viewed as a more global service wherein users from around the world regularly make public their real name and personal photos. These social/cultural trends can be found when browsing through Japanese user profiles.

'Footprints'
On mixi, there is an interesting feature called "ashiato" (footprints) which allows for users to view who has visited their page. This can be a fun feature, because you can figure out which of your friends has taken the most interest in your profile. Since this applies for all users, your activity will be tracked as well. If you have a company page, you can see what types of users have taken an interest in your company.

Search Engine Integration

The last major difference I will mention is the integration of these media into search engine results pages. Mixi, being the purely Japanese platform, doesn't have its pages indexed on Google or Yahoo! Japan. Therefore, you will not see any profiles in the SERPs. Facebook, on the other hand, will show user pages in the SERPs, so it is a more liberal platform in terms of privacy and social media marketing.

	Regis-tered Users	Account Creation	Visit History	"Like-type" Feature	Name	Search Engine Index-ation	Adver-tising Service
Mixi	27.1 million	JP cell phone number needed	Viewable	Yes	Pen names	No	Yes
Face-book	19.6 million	No cell phone number needed	Not viewable	No	Real names	Yes	Yes

As illustrated above, while both mixi and Facebook are similar to each other in the respect that they are SNS, there do exist significant differences between them. It is important to consider these before developing any Japanese social marketing strategies. I hope that this brief introduction to the two platforms will serve as a good reference for your own social marketing campaigns.

The Korean Online Market

		Reference
Population	50,010,000	IMF-World Economic Outlook Database 2012
Internet population	40,329,000	Internet World Stats 2012
Internet use	80%	
Scale of online advertising market	1.8 trillion won	DIGIECO 2012

- Korea is ranked number one in the world for Internet accessibility at 99.3% (Organization for Economic Co-Operation and Development).
- 30% of Internet users read e-books (Arirang News).
- The search engine advertising market in 2011 was valued at 1.1 billion USD, which was equivalent to 68% of the online advertising market (Campaign Brief/Cheil).
- For the year 2011, the e-commerce market was worth 881 million USD. This was a 21.2% increase from 2010 (Statistics Korea).
- 73.1% of Internet users use credit cards for online purchases. 22.8% use money transfers (Statistics Korea).
- 87% of Internet users participate in social media (comScore).

There were 40,329,000 Internet users in Korea in 2012, which comprises 80% of the Korean population. This puts Korea in the top tier of Asian countries with a high level of Internet usage. Korea also has a very high rate of broadband use, which even surpasses the rate in countries like Japan and America.

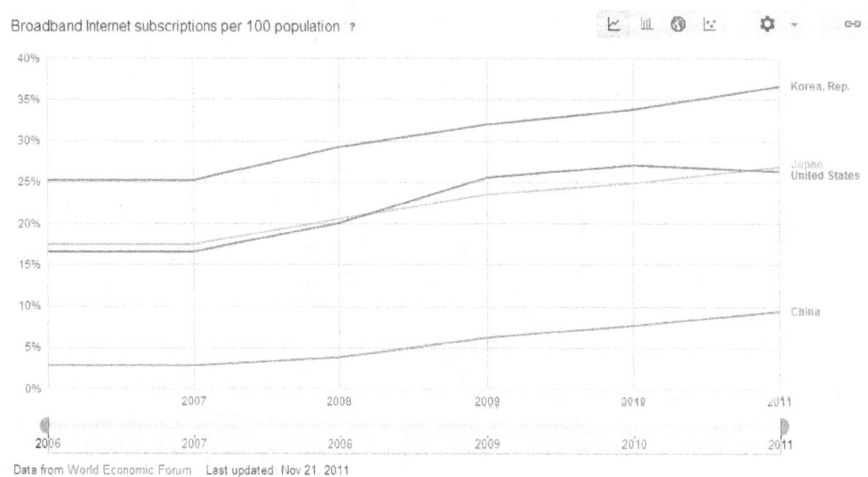

Fig 6.1: Number of broadband Internet subscriptions (per 100 people)

Korea's online advertising market in 2011 was valued at 1.8 trillion won and has sustained an annual growth rate of 20% since then. Online advertising comprises 20% of the total ad market in Korea. The value of the search advertising (e.g. PPC advertising) market in Korea is 1.1 billion USD and dominates 68% of the total online advertising market. Search engine advertising has become an approximately 978 billion won industry, and it has become a common form of advertising among Koreans. Given that search engine advertising's share of the online advertising market has reached the heights it has, it should be part of any online marketing strategy in Korea.

The Korean Search Engine Market
In Korea, the search engine Naver has the highest share of the market at 75.59%. Daum, the second most popular search engine in Korea, has about a 16% share of the market.

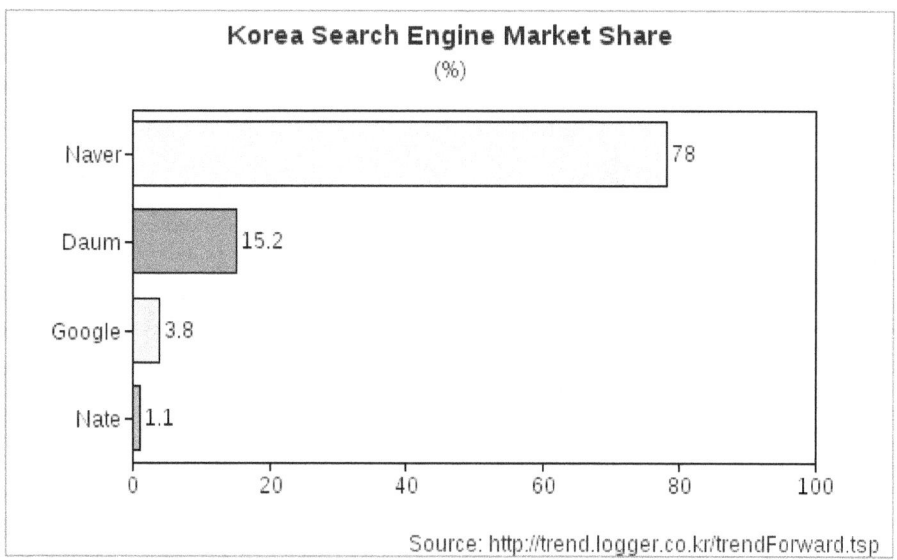

Fig 6.2: Overall search engine shares in Korea

One of the dominant features of Naver is its exceptionally long SERP. Also, the position of content on the page can shift depending on the keyword searched. Some items that will appear on the first page include PPC ads, informative entries based on the searched keyword (the Korean version of Yahoo! Answers), shopping results, Naver Blogs, organic search results, directory sites, Naver Café pages, news, movie information, videos, dictionary entries, and more. Naver's Knowledge iN and blog service often appear in the top area of the SERP, so writing articles for these services could be one way to approach SEO.

Because many Korean search engines, such as Naver, include a wide variety of informational sources on the first SERP, users are accustomed to staying on the first page and accessing only the sites that are presented to them. Thus, among Koreans, traveling to the second page or those further is becoming less common. Due to this phenomenon, having ads appear on the first results page is imperative.

For Naver, the number of spaces available for paid search ads increases and decreases depending on the keyword searched, so we recommend checking your keywords to see what you can expect for availability. This type of search results presentation that is happening among major Korean search engines is called unified search. Simply stated, unified search is a method that involves an analysis of the users' needs associated with searched keywords and the subsequent presentation of different categories based upon these perceived needs.

Naver has two patterns of ranking for their unified search which work in union to display results. The first type of ranking is called collection ranking. This type of ranking pattern shifts the order of major categories on the SERP based on the searched keyword. For example, if you were to search "movie," the category listed at the top of the SERP would be show times. If you were to search "baseball news," on the other hand, blogs or news sites with the most up-to-date news on baseball would be shown. The other type of search pattern Naver implements is its multi-ranking system, which ranks pages within these larger categories.

Google, which has a smaller share of the Korean market, has interestingly customized its SERP appearance for Korean users. The image below exemplifies this unique display. This might be due to the strong influence that Naver has on the search engine market in Korea.

Fig 6.3: A sample Google Korea SERP, customized for Korea

PPC Advertising in Korea

The PPC ad service that Korea's leading search engine, Naver, provides is called "Click Choice." Daum, the second most accessed search engine in Korea, features a service called "Clix." Since Daum only commands a relatively small share of the Korean search engine market, Naver is the recommended PPC advertising service for SEM in Korea.

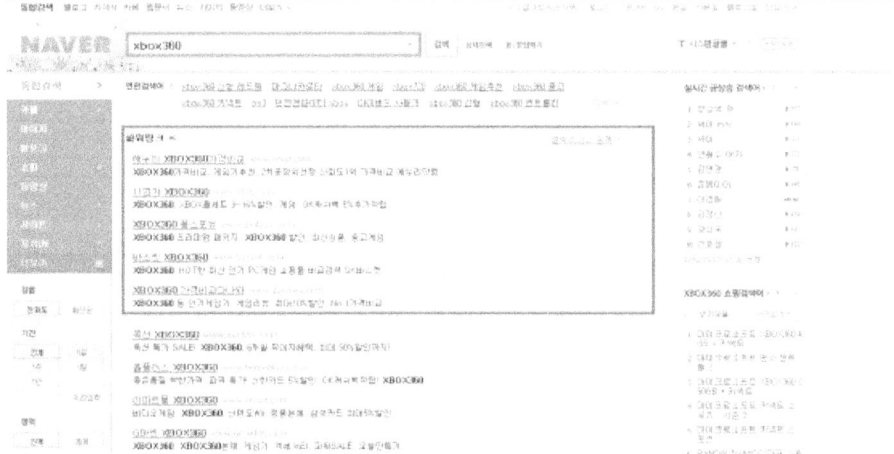

Fig 6.4: The area highlighted above is where Naver's Click Choice ads appear.

Click Choice is Naver's paid search service. The lowest CPC for the service is 70 won (approximately $.06), and bid adjustments can be made in increments of 10 won.

Keyword Type

Click Choice only allows exact match settings for uploaded keywords. Because broad match cannot be utilized, it is important that you think of many keyword variations ahead of time in order to ensure your advertisement will appear as many times as possible. The "exact match" setting means that an ad appears only when the searched keyword <u>exactly</u> matches a keyword registered to the ad. Naver's exact match setting ignores spaces between words. Thus, both "America vacation" and "Americavacation" would bring up the ad associated with that keyword. Naver's exact match also differs from Google in that it will not bring up ads for keywords that have spelling errors or vary orthographically from those that are uploaded. For example, in a search performed for the keyword "Korea travel", the results below would appear:

*   "Koreatravel"
*   "Korea travel"

However, results such as the following wouldn't appear:

*   "Korea travel cheap"
*   "Korea travel riservetion"
*   "travel Korea"

Ad Copy – Character Limits

The character limits for Click Choice ads are a maximum of 15 for the title and 90 for the description (normally there is a 45 character limit for the description, but there is an option of increasing it another 45 characters). The character limits are influenced by the page number on which the ad appears. For the first page, only up to 45 characters for the description will be shown; for pages two and after, up to 90 characters can appear. Since most successful SEM will be done by listing on the first SERP, it is recommended that you construct the ad to not go over the 45 character limit.

전국빠른 꽃배달 119플라워

꽃배달 2시간 빠른배송, 할인된 가격과 마일리지 적립, 계산서발행,

전국당일배송, 회원가입시 7500원 적립, 15%까지 금액을 낮출수 있는 혜택,

http://www.119flower.co.kr/ 광고집행기간 ▬▬▬ ?

Fig 6.5: Example of an ad appearing on the 2nd SERP

The description is two lines and has a character limit of 90. The green bar graph indicates the length of time this ad has been running (the longer the green bar, the longer it has been shown on Naver). It is unclear as to how this graph actually affects viewers.

Ad Copy – Copywriting

Korean PPC ad copy is like those of Western languages in that they tend to insert sentence fragments instead of full sentences to keep messages short and under the character limits. Korean PPC ads are especially to the point, though, and shortening selling points or information about the target promotions as much as possible is a popular tactic.

*   Ad Copy Example:
    Title: 일본여행전문 AA여행사

    Description: 도쿄최저가 30만원. 조기예약 50% 할인. 면세점 쿠폰 제공. 매일 깜짝 이벤트

*   English Translation

    Title: Japan Travel Specialists AA Travel Agency

    Description: Tokyo from 300,000 won. Early reservations 50% off. Coupon gift for Duty Free Store. Specials daily.

The above exemplifies the shortening technique that is characteristic of Korean PPC ads.

The Click Choice Bidding System

Naver's Click Choice bidding system adheres to the following formulae:

*   *Ad rank = bid amount X quality score*
*   *CPC = (next highest score/quality score) + 10 won*

Just like Google or China's Baidu, Naver does not guarantee first rank for ads based solely on the bid amount; it is also important they earn a high quality score. Naver's quality score looks at things such as keyword-ad relevancy, keyword-landing page relevancy, and the CTR of an ad. So, making sure to address these areas when creating campaigns is vital to ensuring a higher score.

Click Choice ads are shown in numerous places, more so than other paid search platforms. Some of these areas include the top area of the SERP, called the "Power Link" area (up to 10 ads can be shown here), the middle area of search results, labeled "Biz Site" (up to five ads can be shown), and in the Naver Knowledge iN and Blog areas (up to three ads). Advertisements on Click Choice can also be shown in other large search networks, which include sites such as Korea's popular shopping site G-Market www.gmarket.co.kr, and auction site www.auction.co.kr. Naver's default settings allow for your PPC ads to be shown in places other than the search results, but if you want to limit your ads to just this area, you must turn the network settings off.

Korean PPC Ad CTRs
Korean PPC ads tend to have high CTRs. One major reason is that keywords are all set to exact match, so they are better aligned with the needs of the searchers. Moreover, Naver thoroughly inspects the keywords and ads that are uploaded onto its PPC platform, so all of the ads have a trustworthy appearance and, thus, attract more clicks.

Brand Advertisements
On Naver, PPC ads are not the only form of advertisement; there are also "Brand Ads," which are special ads that appear for brand name searches. If a user types in a query for a brand name, a large advertisement of that brand will appear at the top of the Naver SERP. These ads can include images or video, too, which make them quite attractive and increase their CTR. These ads are not charged per click. Instead, they are charged by the number of times per month the keywords registered to them are searched. The time frame that these ads can be run is 7-90 days.

Fig 6.5: Naver Brand Advertisement example—it takes up most of the SERP's first view.

The Naver Keyword Tool

Naver has a keyword tool just like Google, so before running any PPC ad campaign, you can analyze the keywords you are considering uploading. In order to gain access to this tool, it is necessary to register for a Naver account. The Naver keyword tool provides category-based keyword search volumes, such as by season or industry. It also provides the number of parties that have bid on a given keyword. Thanks to this feature, the level of competition associated with each keyword can be found out, and planning your bidding strategies for each keyword becomes easier.

Fig 6.6: A screenshot of Naver's keyword tool

Korean SEO

Although for Korean SEO Naver is the search engine of choice (it has the top share in Korea), only three websites are shown in the first page of organic search results. Moreover, as previously explained, Korean users tend to rarely venture to the second page of the search results. For other Korean search engines as well, organic search results are few in number. This seems to be the trend in Korea. For Naver, the position of the organic results can shift depending on the keyword searched, so there is little merit to investing in your website's SEO. Rather, it is important to utilize Naver's services, such as its blog or SNS, in addition to images, videos, and other media in order to gain a stronger presence in the results page.

Blogs are especially popular in Korea, and you will find that they occupy the top area of search results quite often. Consequently, using the Naver blog service to promote your business can be quite an effective online marketing strategy. Just to be sure, we conducted a heavy search in Korea for SEO services and came up with few, if any results. This goes to show that in Korea, SEO is not as important or in demand as it is for other countries. What *is* in demand is marketing through PPC advertising, blogs, and social media.

Website Registration

There is no URL registration page for Naver to rank in its organic search results. Naver, like other search engines, performs constant searches for new links and indexes these pages as they are come across, so there is no need to register your URL on Naver to appear in the SERPs. However, Naver does have a directory service similar to Google Places, which you can take advantage of to possibly get your business higher in the SERPs when relevant. This is definitely a more preferable alternative to a traditional directory. If you are considering this as an option, check out the following link:

*   https://submit.naver.com/

After a directory submission is made, it will take up to a week for your site to appear. It is possible to register sites developed in languages other than Korean, too, but considering that the user base of Naver is Korean, websites in the Korean language are recommended.

Fig 6.7: Naver's directory page—A Korean telephone number is needed in order to register.

Search Engine Directories in Korea

You can also register at the following search engine directories free of charge.

+ Daum: https://register.search.daum.net/index.daum
+ Nate: http://map.nate.com/register/intro.map

The Russian Online Market

		Reference
Population	141,924,000	IMF-World Economic Outlook Database 2012
Internet population	75,645,000	World Bank 2012
Internet use	53.3%	
Scale of online advertising market	41.8 billion rubles	Association of Communication Agencies of Russia

- Russia's most popular SNS is Vkontake (http://vk.com/). Facebook only has a 5% share of the SNS market (Socialbakers).
- Russia is ranked seventh in the world for Internet use (Wikipedia).
- Overall, 73% of Russian citizens aged 18-24 are online, but real usage rates differ by region; Moscow, for example, has a penetration rate of 97% (Yandex and TNS).
- Russia has the highest rate of growth in online sales in all of Europe. From 2010 to 2011, there was a 15.8% increase in e-commerce (comScore).

In 2011, the online advertising market surpassed the print advertising market in Russia. The value of the Russian online market in 2011 was 41.8 billion rubles, which is 55% more than its value one year prior (26.8 billion rubles). The pace at which Russia's online advertising market is growing is remarkable, and many predict that it will continue to grow well into the future.

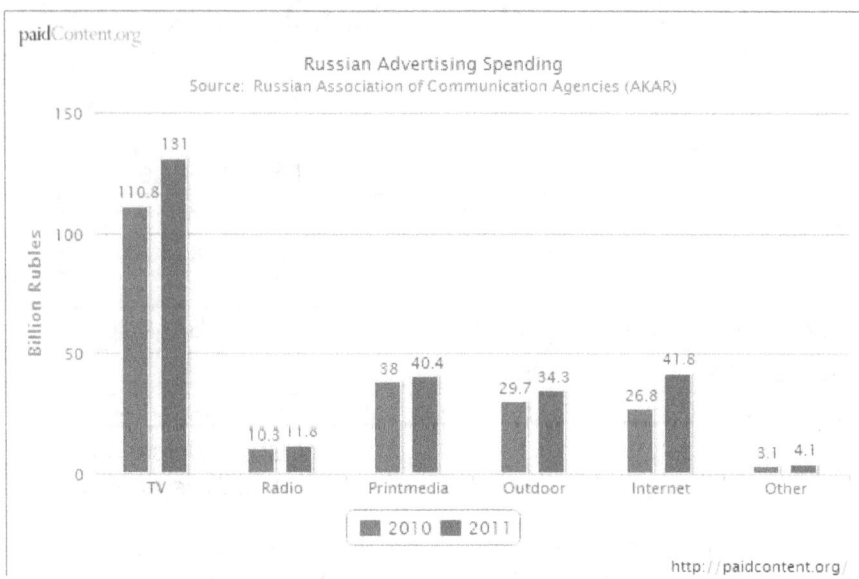

Fig 7.1: Russian advertising spending by medium: following television, online advertising is the second most popular variety of advertising.

The Russian Search Engine Market

In Russia, Yandex has the largest share of the search engine market at 60%, with Google trailing behind at 25%. For SEM in Russia, it is recommended that Yandex be the dominant medium.

Fig 7.2: Yandex's homepage

Yandex commands 64% of Russia's total Internet traffic, which makes it the most popular site in Russia. Yandex is also commonly used for searches in Kazakhstan, Turkey, Ukraine, and Belarus. Yandex is an interesting name; it's actually an acronym-like name meaning "Yet Another iNDEXer." Yandex is used in various countries, but it generally ranks Russian websites higher than those in other languages. Therefore, if you are considering promoting your website on Yandex, it is important to develop a proper Russian website.

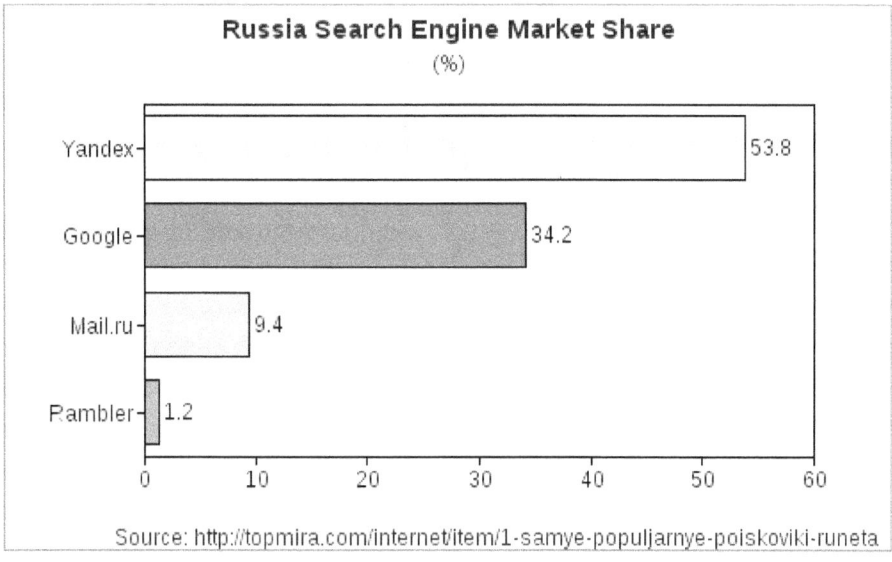

Fig 7.3: Overall search engine shares in Russia

PPC Advertising in Russia

In Russia, the two main platforms for PPC advertising are Yandex Direct and Google AdWords. If you happen to already have a Google AdWords account, then you are definitely able to start advertising in Russia; however, given Google's market share in Russia is only 34%, Yandex Direct is naturally the preferred advertising medium.

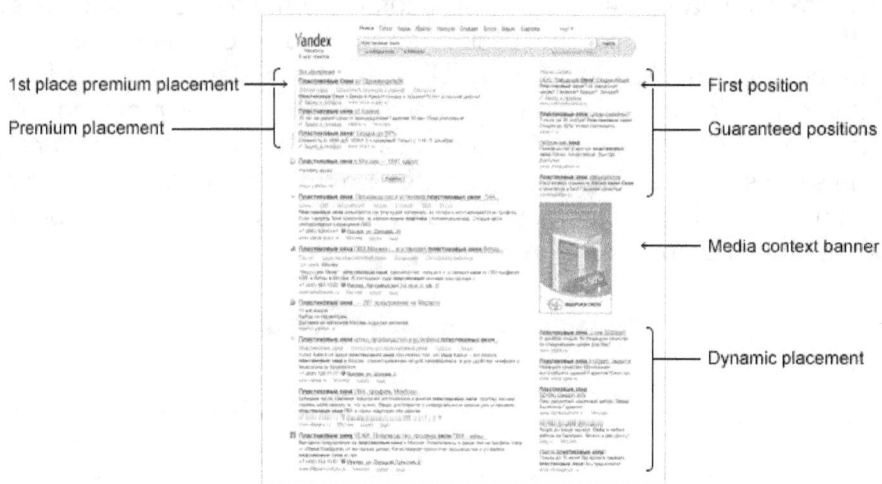

1st place premium placement ⟶ ⟵ First position

Premium placement ⟶ ⟵ Guaranteed positions

⟵ Media context banner

⟵ Dynamic placement

Fig 7.4: A Yandex SERP—Like Yahoo! or Google, ads appear on the top of the page and on the right hand side.

Fortunately, in addition to Russian, Yandex Direct also provides its paid search advertising platform in English. Don't worry. There is hope for those not versed in the Russian language.

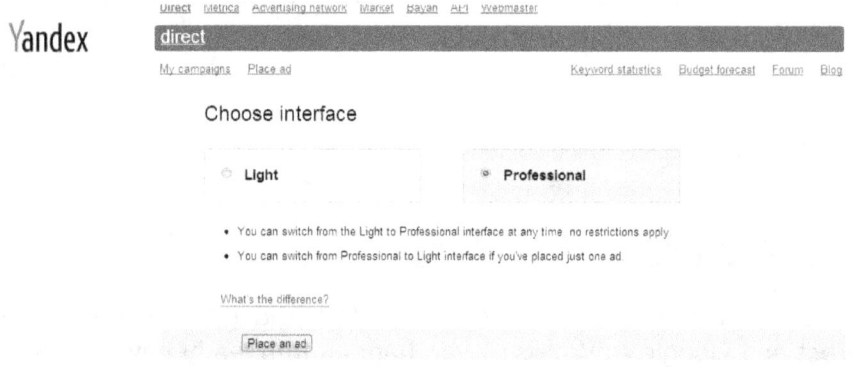

Fig 7.5: The Yandex account creation screen

When you create an account on Yandex Direct, you can choose between a "Light" and a "Professional" version. The Professional version operates just like an AdWords account; the Light version, on the other hand, is built for those just starting their paid search advertising journey. For the Light version, many functions are limited. No matter which version you decide to sign up for, you can always switch to the other at a later time, so there is not much cause for concern. What I recommend, though, is to start with the Light version until you get used to its format and functions, then switch over to the Professional one.

Bidding on Yandex

On Yandex, you can start advertising with bids as low as 30 kopecks, but you will need to set up the account with an initial budget of 300 rubles. As for the bidding features, they are similar to that of Google AdWords, such as having the ability to adjust according to geographic location or time. When bidding on keywords, Yandex used to only allow those with CTRs above 0.5%, but this has recently changed, and now keywords of various CTRs can be bid on. The only catch is that the keywords with low CTRs will generally have higher CPCs. In order to avoid high bid prices and still increase your ranking, it is recommended you amend or delete keywords and ads with low CTRs.

Quality Factor and Efficiency Factor

Yandex has two indices that work cooperatively to determine a minimum CPC -- the "Quality Factor" and the "Efficiency Factor." There are many elements that comprise these two indices, with certain factors outweighing others. The main components of the Quality Factor are keyword and ad relevancy, ad and landing page relevancy, and ad performance. The Efficiency Factor, on the other hand, looks at ad impression, CTR, and the period of time an ad runs. These factors are all analyzed in real time and combined to calculate a minimum CPC for an ad.

Ad Copy

Text ads on Yandex have to conform to the following specifications:
- Title -- up to 33 characters
- Description -- up to 75 characters

Some of the information you cannot insert into ads includes phone numbers, e-mail addresses, physical addresses, instant messenger data, and other sensitive information.

The top three ad spots on the Yandex SERPs are considered the premium area, and the format of the ads looks like this:

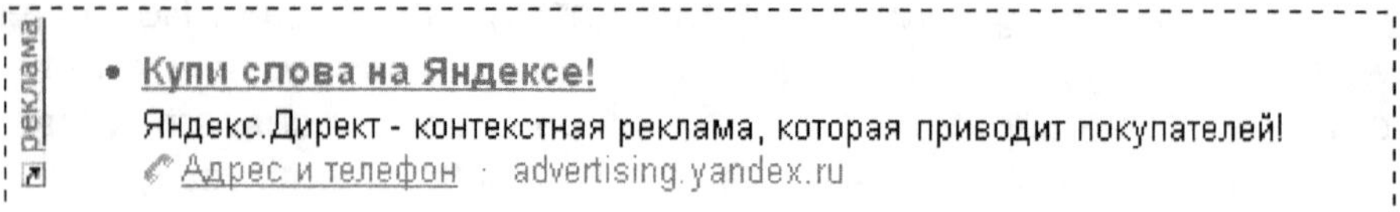

- **Купи слова на Яндексе!**
  Яндекс.Директ - контекстная реклама, которая приводит покупателей!
  Адрес и телефон · advertising.yandex.ru

Fig 7.6: Ads for premium position

If an ad falls below the third position, however, it will appear on the right side of the SERP and take on the following appearance:

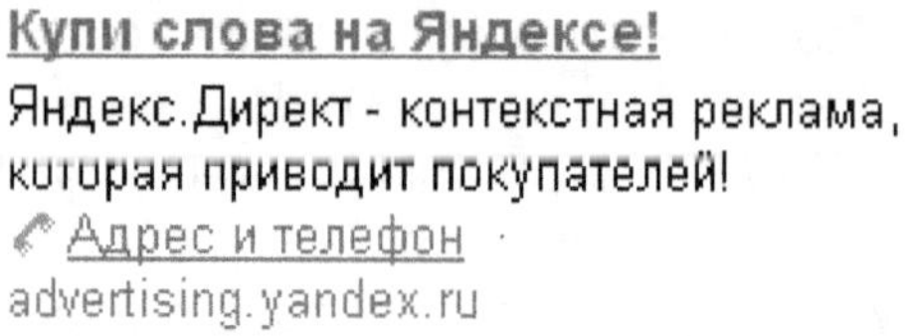

Купи слова на Яндексе!
Яндекс.Директ - контекстная реклама, которая приводит покупателей!
Адрес и телефон ·
advertising.yandex.ru

Fig 7.7: Ads for basic position

The CTRs for ads in the premium area and the right side are also significantly different. Since ads with low CTRs still run the possibility of being paused by Yandex, it is best to aim for appearing in the premium area.

Yandex's Advertising Regulations can be found here:

- http://legal.yandex.com/direct_adv_rules/

Match Type

For the most part, the match type for Yandex Direct is the same as for Google AdWords. There are minor differences though; for example, Google AdWords exact match is designated by brackets ([used cars]), while Yandex uses quotation marks ("used cars"). Furthermore, Yandex's exact match type will display the singular and plural version of a keyword ("used cars" or "used car"), but AdWords won't. Overall, it is best to exercise caution when designating match type if you are used to Google and just starting out on Yandex.

Information on Yandex's match type can be found here:

- http://www.russiansearchtips.com/2011/10/match-types-in-yandex-explained/

Tips on increasing the effectiveness of your SEM campaigns on Yandex can be found on the official site:

- Regularly A/B test your ads to increase your CTRs.
- Adjust your keywords based on performance and add or delete keywords as necessary.
- Eliminate keywords with low CTRs.
- Use the Yandex Autobroker Tool to improve your ads and your CPC.
- Use Yandex's Autofocus feature to improve the CTR of your keywords.
- Adjust your advertising locations accordingly.
- Adjust your advertising times.
- Put actual prices in your ad copy.

Regional Settings

Russia is a very large country. Thus, you can expect different levels of performance by region. For Russian SEM, it is recommended you utilize Yandex's regional settings to the best of your abilities so that you can increase your performance. Two locations you cannot afford bypassing are Moscow and St. Petersburg. These cities have great access to quality ISPs, so rather precise targeting can be performed. Yandex also allows targeting for countries other than Russia, but it is limited to only a few neighboring countries. Since Yandex's share in these places isn't exceptionally large, it is best to keep your location settings to just Russia.

Selection of regions for ad shows

You can refine the region in which your ads are shown to inc
(according to our database), as well as those who have sel

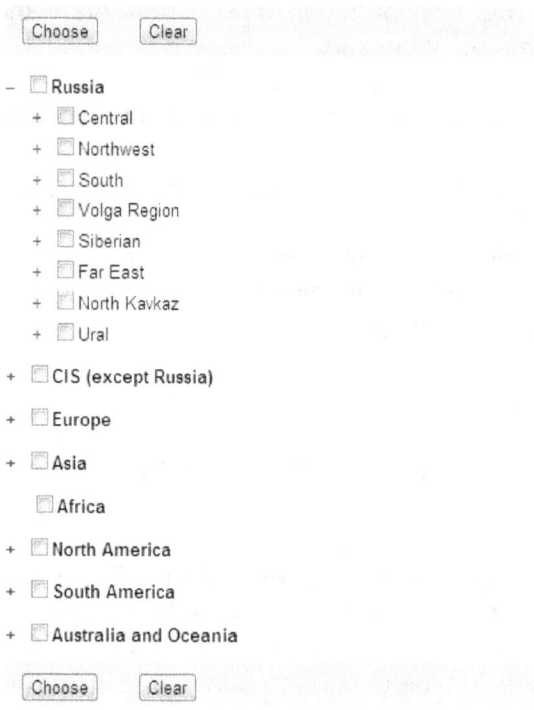

Fig 7.8: You can target specific regions within Russia.

Differences in Yandex and Google's CTR

According to research by Neiron.ru, the top three ad placements on Yandex (premium positions) have a combined average CTR of 75.5%, where the same three positions on Google.ru command an overall CTR of 91.1%. This shows that for Google, more than for Yandex, it is important to be in the top three positions if you want an increase in site traffic.

Fig 7.9: CTR per ad position on Yandex
Source: http://neiron.ru/

Fig 7.10: CTR per ad position on Google.ru
Source: http://neiron.ru/

The Yandex Keyword Tool

Yandex has a keyword tool named "Wordstat," which can be used to investigate keyword search volume and keyword trends:

- http://wordstat.yandex.ru/

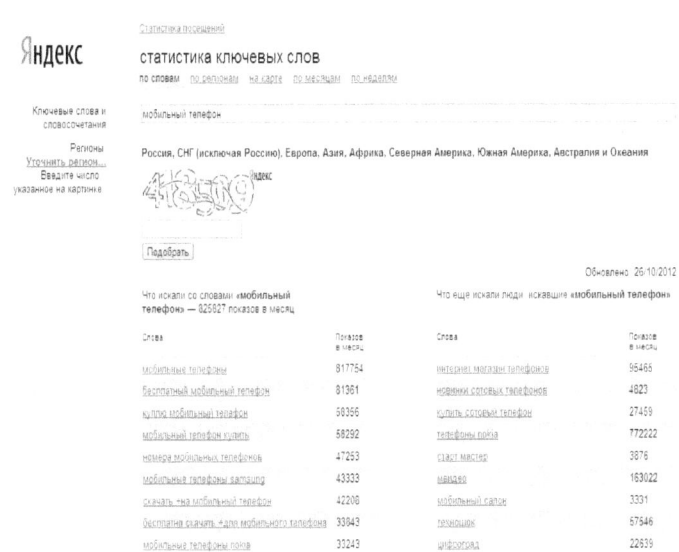

Fig 7.11: Wordstat by Yandex—Keyword search volumes and other data are available

Using the Yandex keyword tool, Wordstat, you can research monthly keyword search volumes, regional keyword search data, related keywords, and weekly differences in search volume; there's even a map display of keyword data. Yandex's data is constantly being refreshed, and there is a large variety to take advantage of. So, I would say Wordstat is a must-use tool for your Russian paid search campaigns on Yandex.

Tracking Conversions

One surprising thing about Yandex Direct is that it does not have a conversion tracking feature. In order to track conversions, you must use Metrika, Yandex's version of Google Analytics (Metrika will be explained in more detail later). Fortunately, this tool can be linked to Yandex Direct, so you can track conversions. Tracking conversions is essential to measuring your advertising expenditure and performance, so Metrika, or Google Analytics at the very least, needs to be integrated into your campaigns.

Russian SEO

Search engine optimization in Russia is generally performed on Yandex or Google.ru. Since Yandex prefers Russian language content to that of other languages, first and foremost you will need a Russian language website in order to have hopes of ranking higher. Besides, Russian is the national language of Russia, and so most commerce on the Internet is conducted in it.

Yandex's Thematic Citation Index

One of the characteristics of Yandex is that it has its own system of scoring websites, similar to something like Google's PageRank. And, it ultimately is influential in ranking search results. Yandex calls this its Thematic Citation Index (TCI), and it is a good indicator of the trustworthiness of a website. The TCI analyzes numerous elements of a site when attributing a score, which is eventually used for ranking purposes, but Yandex considers links for its ranking as well. For SEO on Yandex, it is important to have backlinks, or for you to link to, sites that are highly relevant to yours.

Yandex's TCI scores websites from 0 to 150,000. Generally speaking, the higher the TCI, the higher ranking a site will have on the SERPs. However, like Google's PageRank, this is not always the case. That is why it is important to invest in your website's internal and external SEO, too. Ensuring a high quality site with relevant links from equally high quality sites will raise your TCI score and other factors which improve your ranking.

TCI is comprised of the following elements:

- The number of backlinks
- The quality of your backlinks (i.e. linked site's domain age, linked site's own number of backlinks)
- The relevancy of your backlinks (e.g. for used auto sales, links from sites related to the automobile market have a high relevancy)
- The TCI score of sites linked to yours (the higher the score, the better)

- The quality of your site's content (e.g. content that users will find informative and helpful)
- The types of sites you link to (e.g. how many relevant sites you are linking to)
- The number of links in your site
- Link pattern analysis (i.e. checks to make sure your links are not uniformly set, as would be the case for systematic link building)
- Geographical hosting information
- How many days you have been registered in the Yandex Catalog (Yandex Catalog is Yandex's search engine directory)

1. How to look up your TCI score
There is more than one way to look up your own site's TCI:

- Yandex Catalog (Yandex's directory)
- Yandex Toolbar (http://bar.yandex.ru/)
- Yandex Webmaster Tools

Domains
While I stated previously that it is important to have a Russian language site for SEO in Russia, having a Russian domain is also key to ensuring a higher ranking. I highly recommend acquiring a Russian country code top-level domain (ccTLD), as Yandex will value it over foreign counterparts. It is a great first step to improving your site's SEO.

Metadata
For Yandex, just like other search engines, you want to make sure your website's metadata is optimized for SEO. Yandex especially values the title tag. The length of your pages' title tags should not go over 70 characters, and they should definitely include your target keywords.

The meta description tag, on the other hand, should be around 150-160 characters in length. For these tags, it is important that you not only include target keywords, but also write an accurate and appealing description that will lead to more visits to your site. However, like Google, Yandex will first crawl your page and decide whether your meta description is good enough to display in its SERPs. When it isn't, Yandex will create a snippet to show as your site's description. This is done by selecting excerpts of text from your web page and combining them to create a paragraph description of the page. In order to bypass this feature of Yandex, it is important to write your descriptions accurately, stylistically, and informatively, all within the recommended character limit.

For the meta keyword tag, although Yandex doesn't disregard it like Google (for the most part) does, it doesn't place much importance on it overall. Regardless, it's a good idea to include your target keywords in your keywords tag, just in case. The maximum number should be five or six.

Yandex Catalog Registration

Yandex has its own directory site that you can submit your website to. For SEO on Yandex, it is recommended you submit your site to its directory; just by registering, your TCI will increase. The Yandex Catalog has both paid and free registration. The paid version has a one-time application fee of 12,500 rubles (about 390 USD). Upon payment, your site will be investigated, and after a few days, will be posted on the Yandex Catalog. Acceptance is not guaranteed though, so make sure to develop a high quality Russian language site with plenty of rich content so that you can pass the Yandex inspection. One word of caution is that the application fee of 12,500 rubles is non-refundable, so it is important you develop a quality site. The other option is to go the free route, but the drawback here is that your site can take months to be inspected, and if it eventually fails the examination, you will have to start the process all over again.

Fig 7.12: Yandex Catalog—The largest Russian directory

Free submission to the Yandex Catalog can be found here:

- http://yaca.yandex.ru/add_free.xml

If you are curious as to why Yandex names its directory "Catalog," it is because in Russia, search engine directories are called "catalogs."

1. Other Search Engine Directories in Russia

- http://list.mail.ru/index.html
- http://top100.rambler.ru/

Website Registration

Website URL registration can be done through the link below. Registering on this site is recommended, as it will speed up the indexation of your website. However, whether your site is indexed or not is up to Yandex, so there are no guarantees. Also, it will not affect the ranking of your site.

- http://webmaster.yandex.com/addurl.xml

Yandex Webmaster Tools

Yandex also has its own version of Webmaster Tools, which will provide you a plethora of data about your site. Yandex's Webmaster Tools is functionally very similar to Google's, with features such as site map registration, search for error pages, and link analysis. Just like Google's Webmaster Tools, in order to be able to use the service, webmasters will have to insert Yandex's tags within their pages' source code and get verified.

The Taiwanese Online Market

		Reference
Population	23,316,000	IMF-World Economic Outlook Database 2012
Internet population	17,530,000	Internet World Stats 2012
Internet use	75.4%	
Scale of online advertising market	346 million USD	IAMA

- There is an 82% rate of Internet use among Taiwanese housewives (Institute for Information Industry).
- The results of an investigation found that Taiwanese access the Internet mostly for news (29.9%), then entertainment (23.3%), consumption (14.4%), work-related issues (12.6%), travel (10.4%), and finally financial matters (10.1%) (RDEC).
- The paid search market is valued at 3 billion TWD and is growing more than 15% a year. It comprises 30.1% of the online advertising market (IAMA).
- Business-to-Consumer based e-commerce in Taiwan is worth 8.33 billion USD and is growing each year by 25% (China Economic News Service).
- Apparel is the number one type of online purchase in Taiwan (The China Post).
- 67% of Taiwanese Internet users refer to social media before making their online purchases. And, after they have made their purchases, 50% of them will use social media to express their opinion on the product or service they bought (FIND-III DoIT).
- 71.4% of Taiwanese Internet users have their own Facebook account (Socialbakers).

Internet use in Taiwan is at 75.4% of the total population, which is relatively high compared to other countries. The search engine advertising market in Taiwan is growing at a rate of 15% each year and is forecasted to continue do so into the future.

In Taiwan, Chinese is the spoken language and the main language of advertising; however, it differs from mainland Chinese in that traditional characters are used instead of their simplified counterparts. When planning to market online in the greater China region, a site that incorporates traditional Chinese characters will have to be developed for Taiwan.

The Taiwanese Search Engine Market

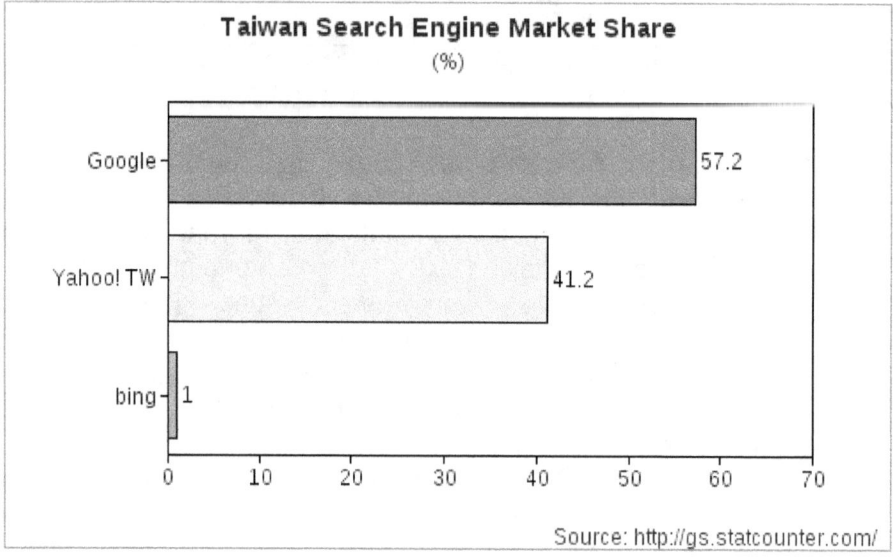

Fig 8.1: Overall search engine shares in Taiwan

Taiwan is one of the countries in the world that still has a large percentage of users on Yahoo! performing their daily searches. The market share that Google has in Taiwan is only around 57%, so when considering SEM in Taiwan, it is best to advertise on both platforms. Baidu, on the other hand, which commands the largest share of the Chinese market, only has captured a mere 1% in Taiwan. Consequently, for SEM in the greater China region, Taiwan should be considered separately from the mainland.

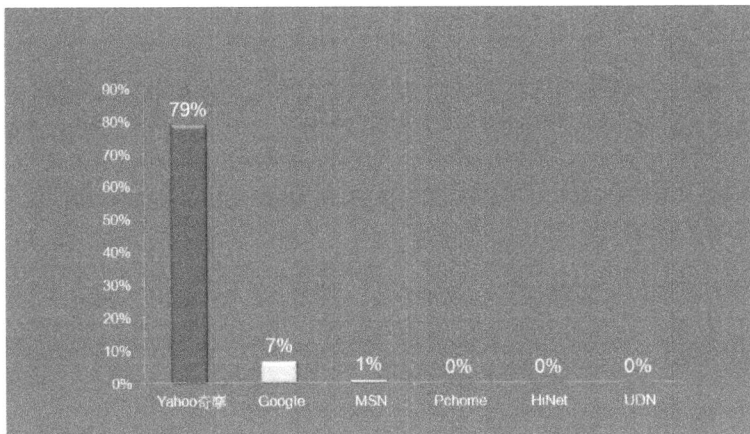

Fig 8.2: Home page setting for internet browsers in Taiwan (percentages).

Source: Nielsen Media Research, 2011

In Taiwan, 79% of Internet users have set Yahoo! Taiwan as their home page. This shows how influential Yahoo! is in Taiwan.

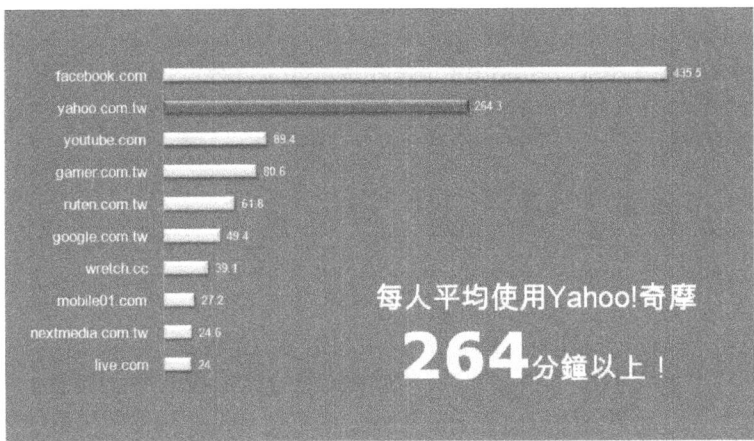

Fig 8.3: Average time spent on websites by Taiwanese Internet users
Source: InsightXplorer ARO Report, Jan. 2012

As the graph above illustrates, Yahoo! Taiwan is second only to Facebook for the longest amount of time spent per site visit (264 minutes).

PPC Advertising in Taiwan

In Taiwan, the paid search advertising market is split largely between Google and Yahoo! Taiwan. Since Taiwan's population is approximately 23,000,000 people in size (a comparatively small market), it is recommended that both Yahoo! Taiwan and Google are used for any paid search campaigns.

	Google AdWords	Yahoo! Taiwan
Ad title	15 characters (2 byte) / 30 characters (1 byte)	15 characters (2 byte) / 30 characters (1 byte)
Ad description	19 characters (2 byte) / 38 characters (1 byte)	38 characters (2 byte) / 76 characters (1 byte)

Taiwan uses traditional Chinese characters for its writing system, which makes it a 2-byte language digitally. For 2-byte languages, there are different PPC ad character limits than those whose script only has 1-byte characters. Yahoo! Taiwan and Google AdWords also differ in this area. Yahoo! Taiwan allows twice the number of characters to be entered into the description as what is permitted on Google AdWords. Yahoo! Taiwan PPC ads are therefore able to convey more information to search engine users, which can lead to higher CTRs than the Google counterparts.

Yahoo! Taiwan PPC: Characteristics

One characteristic of Yahoo! Taiwan's paid search platform that is beneficial for non-Chinese speakers is that it can be displayed in English. Another important (and cautionary) characteristic about the Yahoo! Taiwan paid search platform is that there is a three-month suspension imposed on PPC campaigns if switches are made in SEM agency. Therefore, when considering which SEM agency will manage your Yahoo! Taiwan PPC campaign, it is imperative you thoroughly investigate their background and see if they truly have the ability to provide you the quality of service and performance you desire.

Traditional and Simplified Chinese:

Differences It is important to always keep in mind the difference between traditional and simplified Chinese characters when planning your paid search campaigns in Taiwan. It doesn't simply stop at the script, though; there are myriad differences between the vernacular of Chinese spoken in Taiwan and that of the mainland. Consider the word "yogurt" as a simple example. In China it is pronounced /suān nǎi/ and written酸奶, but in Taiwan it's /yōu gé/ and written優格. It is recommended that you check your ad copy and keywords with a native Taiwanese before uploading them to your campaigns, even if you have checked a Chinese-English translation tool or dictionary. You can't expect great results if your Taiwanese ad copy is written in simplified Chinese or a vernacular from the mainland. It's always best to get a native's opinion.

Taiwanese SEO

In the same fashion as paid search advertising, the target media for SEO in Taiwan are Yahoo! and Google. For Yahoo! Taiwan, though, it must be noted that it is currently using Microsoft's Bing. Therefore, in order to optimize for both Google and Yahoo! Taiwan, similarities must be found between Google and Bing's algorithms.

SEO on Bing

Bing, like Google, ranks websites higher if they contain rich content and backlinks from high quality, relevant sites. Listed below are some SEO tips for Bing.

1. Bing Webmaster Tools Registration The first step to doing SEO on Bing is
registering for a Bing Webmaster Tools account. (http://www.bing. com/toolbox/ webmaster). Numerous features are available to help you analyze your data, so it is highly recommended that you create an account. It is OK to register most any language's site, since Bing's Webmaster Tools is universal.

2. Site Map Setting For SEO on Bing, it is particularly important for you to register
your website's site map. This can also be done using Bing Webmaster Tools. Compared to Google, Bing tends to be weaker in its ability to index websites. Therefore, it is very important to register a solid site

map so that Bing's robot can crawl your site properly. Make sure to register every page you want indexed in your site map.

3. Utilizing the SEO Analyzer and SEO Report
Bing's Webmaster Tools also contains
an SEO analysis element (in the beta version at time of this book's writing). This tool can help one perform fundamental SEO for his/her site. Using it, you can identify all the various SEO problems your site is facing and ultimately get the information you need to improve it.

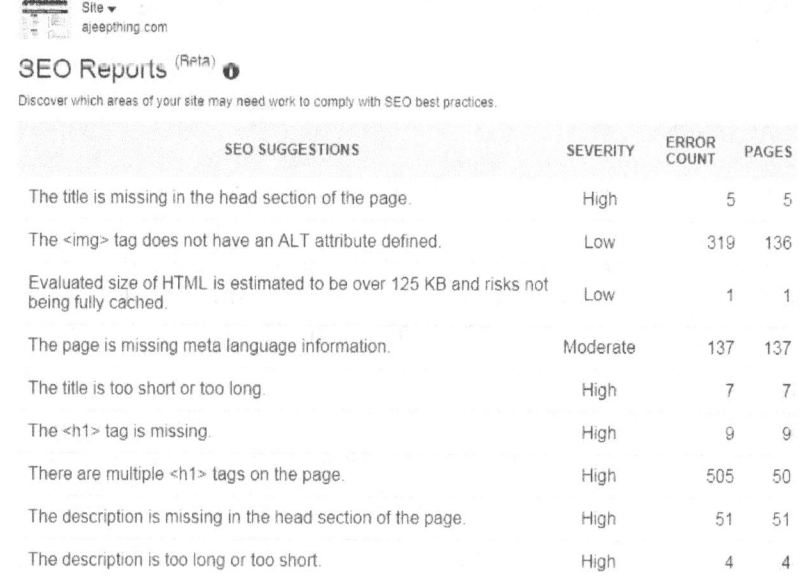

Fig 9.4: A screenshot of Bing's SEO Reports, wherein fundamental SEO suggestions and error reporting are provided

4. Link Building
For Google and Bing, it is important to develop link building

strategies. This is naturally important for Taiwan, too. One point not to forget for your Taiwanese SEO, though, is that it is important to make sure your backlinks are from sites with the same traditional Chinese characters. In Taiwan, paid link services are not easy to come by (most search engines forbid them anyway), so you will need to earn as many links as possible from contextually relevant sites that have the same language in order to strengthen your link portfolio and increase your ranking.

Google AdWords and Yahoo! Taiwan: Keyword Data

Contrary to Google, Yahoo! Taiwan has a keyword tool that can be used even if a user doesn't have a paid search account. For Google AdWords, if you have an account, you can alter the language and country search options to extract the keyword data you need for your Taiwanese SEM campaigns.

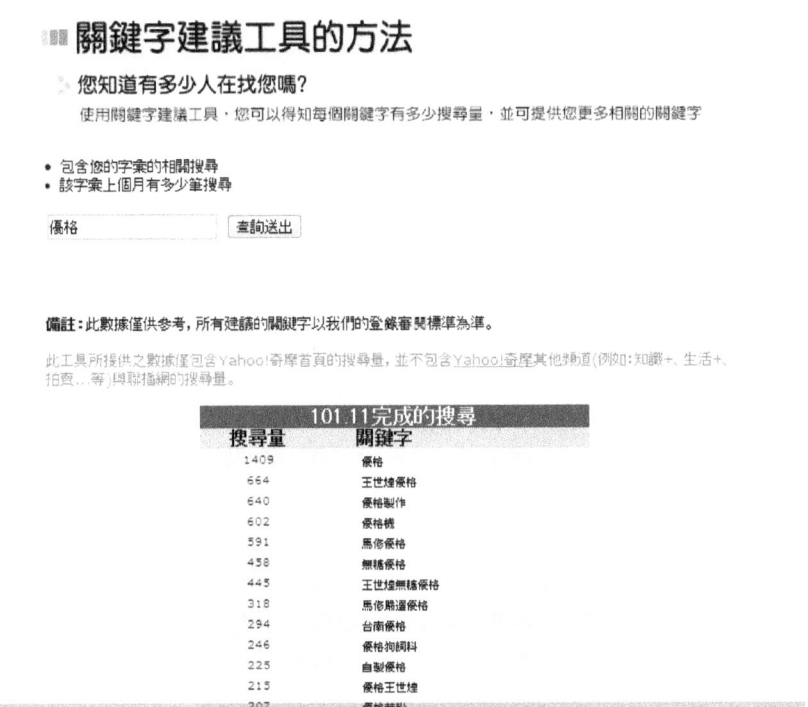

Fig 9.5: Yahoo! Taiwan's keyword tool

Its interface might bring back memories for those of you who have been in paid search since the early days: http://tw.emarketing.yahoo.com/ysm/guide/index101.html

Search Engine Directories in Taiwan

- http://www.thiu.org.tw/
  Registration page: http://www.thiu.org.tw/add-w.htm
- http://www.directory.com.tw
  Registration page: http://www.directory.com.tw/members/user_register.php
- http://www.yam.com/

More Tips About Taiwan

Yahoo! Taiwan also features other types of online ads. Here I will introduce a couple.

Run of Network Ads Run of Network (RON) ads are advertisements with special placements that only Yahoo! Taiwan partner agencies can sell. These ads can appear in areas such as the Yahoo! Taiwan top page, news, money, dictionary, and blog pages. These are pay-per-click type ads, so you will only be charged if they are clicked on. Depending on the position of the ad, the number of impressions can vary from a million to tens of millions of appearances per day. The lowest possible CPC for this type of ad is 10 TWD (.34 USD), and they can be run from 5,000 TWD (about 170 USD) a day. This type of ad is different from a general paid search ad in that it has a broader reach, which can be great for introducing new products or strengthening your brand.

The Hong Kongese Online Market

		Reference
Population	7,173,000	IMF–World Economic Outlook Database 2012
Internet population	5,329,000	www. internetworldstats. com 2012
Internet use	74.2%	
Scale of online advertising market	91 million USD	SMB World Asia Edition

- HK$1.86 billion was used in advertising for Chinese New Year in 2012 (online and offline). This is 6.7% of the cumulative average yearly expenditure (Asia Media Journal).
- According to a 2011 Google study, 78% of smartphone users saw ads and clicked on them. (Publicitas).
- The online retail market in 2011 was 1.9 billion USD, and it has been estimated that it will grow to 2.5 billion USD by 2015 (PayPal/Enterprise Innovation).
- 37% of the population banks online (Nielsen).
- For the population of Hong Kong, mobile phones have a 225.5% penetration rate (Office of the Communications Authority 2012).

Hong Kong's population is only 7,130,000, but 74.3% of it is online. It has one of the more active online markets in Asia. Comparing television and Internet use for the years 2006 and 2010, it becomes clear that TV viewership has fallen over time, and Internet use has increased significantly.

Time Spent per Day Online & Watching T.V. (Mins & Percentage Change)

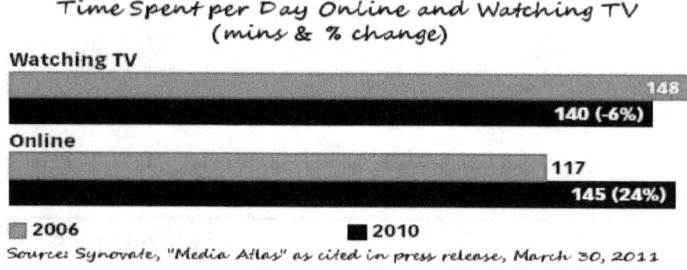

Fig 9.1: A simultaneous drop in TV viewership and rise in Internet use occurred between 2006 and 2010.

Foreign corporations that cannot host their websites in China often set up shop in Hong Kong. Due to China's restrictions, the number of these types of companies has multiplied in recent years.

In Hong Kong, both Cantonese and English are official languages. English, in particular, is used quite often in business as a large portion of business conducted in Hong Kong is with overseas companies. With regard to Cantonese, it is important to note that, like Taiwan, Hong Kong uses traditional Chinese characters, not the simplified versions used in the mainland.

The Hong Kongese Search Engine Market

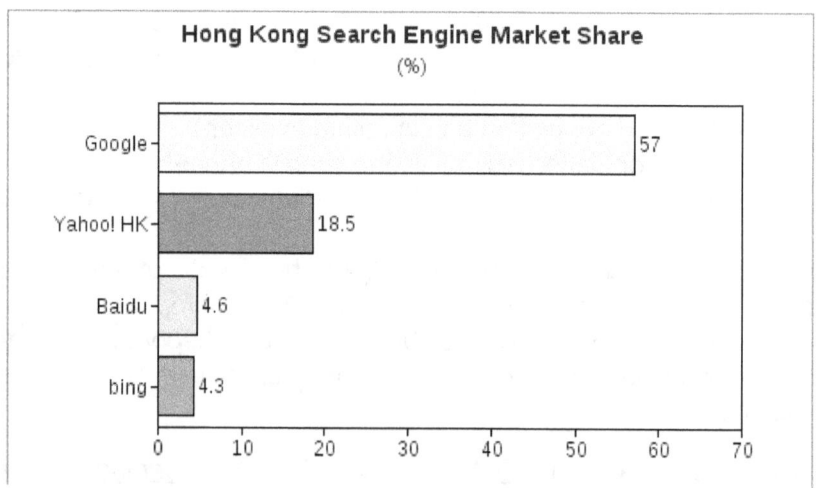

Fig 9.2: Overall search engine shares in Hong Kong

Baidu, which commands the top share for search engines in China, has only captured 3.58% of the overall search engine share in Hong Kong. Thus, it is important to consider China and Hong Kong independently when developing an online marketing strategy for the greater China area.

PPC Advertising in Hong Kong

Before running SEM campaigns in Hong Kong, it is necessary to choose which language you will use as your ads' target language. As previously stated, English and Cantonese are both official languages, and, thus, both are potential languages in which to advertise.

Consider the data below, wherein searches in English and Cantonese (traditional characters) were performed for "used car," "credit card," and "insurance."

Keyword (by relevance)	Avg. monthly searches ?	Competition ?	Suggested bid ?
used car	260	High	$0.66
二手車	6,600	Medium	$0.26

Fig 9.3: "Used Car" monthly search volumes for Hong Kong

Keyword (by relevance)	Avg. monthly searches ?	Competition ?	Suggested bid ?
insurance	1,900	High	$11.12
保險	1,900	High	$4.29

Fig 9.4: "Insurance" monthly search volumes for Hong Kong

Keyword (by relevance)	Avg. monthly searches ?	Competition ?	Suggested bid ?
credit card	2,400	High	$2.97
信用卡	3,600	High	$2.35

Fig 9.5: "credit card" monthly search volumes for Hong Kong

As the screen captures above show, suggested bid price can fluctuate significantly depending upon language. In the example of the keyword "Insurance", the English bid price is over twice the amount of its Chinese counterpart. This helps to illustrate the important point of researching which language is best for a paid search campaign in Hong Kong.

Hong Kongese SEO

Google's search engine market share in Hong Kong is the highest at 60%, so it is natural that SEO be conducted in light of Google's algorithms. In second place is Yahoo! Hong Kong, which currently is being powored by Microsoft's Bing, so if ranking high on Yahoo! Hong Kong is preferred, optimizing websites to the Bing algorithms is ideal (SEO tips for Bing are explained in the Taiwan chapter). Regarding link building, while it is ideal to keep things local by using as many as possible from domestic websites, Hong Kong has a relatively small number of sites when compared to other countries, making difficult to build an effective portfolio. In order to get as many links from as many relevant domains as possible, producing quality, attractive content is key, for it will likely lead to content sharing and the formation of multiple backlinks to your site.

More Information about Hong Kong

Apple Daily is a well-known Hong Kongese portal site.

Fig 9.6: Apple Daily, one of Hong Kong's most well-known portal sites
(http://hk.apple.nextmedia.com/)

The number of companies running display ads on Apple Daily has increased dramatically since 2009. This puts Apple Daily in position to possibly meet or surpass Yahoo! in the near future.

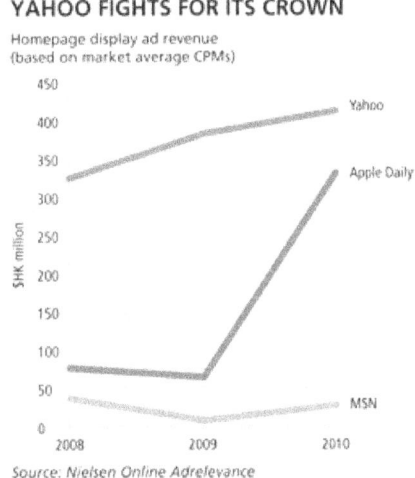

Fig 9.7: Apple Daily has been increasing its advertising share rapidly in recent years.

The Singaporean Online Market

		Reference
Population	5,405,000	IMF-World Economic Out-look Database 2012
Internet population	3,650,000	Internet World Stats 2012
Internet use	67.5%	
Scale of online adver-tising market	S$135.91 (107 million USD)	Interactive Advertising Bureau 2011

* Approximately 62% of the Singapore population is on Facebook (Socialbakers).
* Among Singapore's Internet population, 80% of users utilize Facebook (Socialbakers).
* The size of Singapore's 2010 online shopping market was 1.1 billion SGD, and it has been estimated that it will quadruple by 2015 (PayPal 2011).
* In 2011, Singapore's total number of online searches per month reached approximately 300 million. Compared to 2010, that is a 43% increase (comScore 2011).
* The number of broadband circuits in 2011 reached 9.22 million, 7.9 million of which were high speed wireless Internet networks (IDA).
* Singaporeans spend an average of 25 hours per week on the Internet (Nielsen).

Increasingly, Singapore is being considered as the hub of Asia. While it only has a population of about 5 million, 71% use the Internet, which means Singapore is one of the more Internet savvy countries in Asia.

In Singapore, there are four commonly used languages: English, Simplified Chinese, Malay, and Tamil. Consequently, when planning to market online in Singapore, one must first choose which language to focus on. In terms of the ethnic makeup of the country, the following three groups comprise the majority of the population: Chinese (74%), Malaysian (13%), and Indian (9.2%). Given the fact that, in Singapore, all schools use English as their language of instruction and Singaporeans understand the language well, there is good enough reason to develop websites in English. It is said that 36% of the population is made up of foreigners, so this also argues for using English for website development. Since 74% of the population is ethnically Chinese, though, the Chinese language is another viable alternative or addition to English.

According to research conducted by PayPal in 2011, from 2010 to 2015, the online shopping market in Singapore is expected to grow approximately four times its current scale. When looking at the 2010 online sales data by industry, the travel sector had the highest figures at 307 million SGD, which is 28% of the online shopping market. Another interesting piece of data pertaining to e-commerce is that Internet users in Singapore use domestic websites and foreign websites differently when shopping online. When purchasing things such as insurance or event tickets, Singaporean websites are mainly used, but when purchasing books or other forms of entertainment, such as music or games, foreign websites are preferred. Additionally, for apparel, more than 50% of online purchases are made on foreign websites.

Category	Market Scale	Share
Travel	307 million SGD	28%
Fashion/Beauty	146 million SGD	13%
Entertainment/Lifestyle	143 million SGD	13%
IT/Electronics	83 million SGD	11%
Insurance	83 million SGD	7%

Reference:

http://www.mediabuzz.com.sg/asian-emarketing-latest-issue/1247-paypals-first-comprehensive-study-on-online-and-mobile-shopping-in-singapore

The Singaporean Search Engine Market
In Singapore, Google has the highest share of the market at 86.51%. And, since English is a first language for most of the citizens, searches in English are growing in number. The scale of the SEM market in 2008 was 2.8 million SGD; however, in 2010 it reached 15.9 million SGD, which means in only three years' time, it grew five times its original size (Ref: mvfglobal).

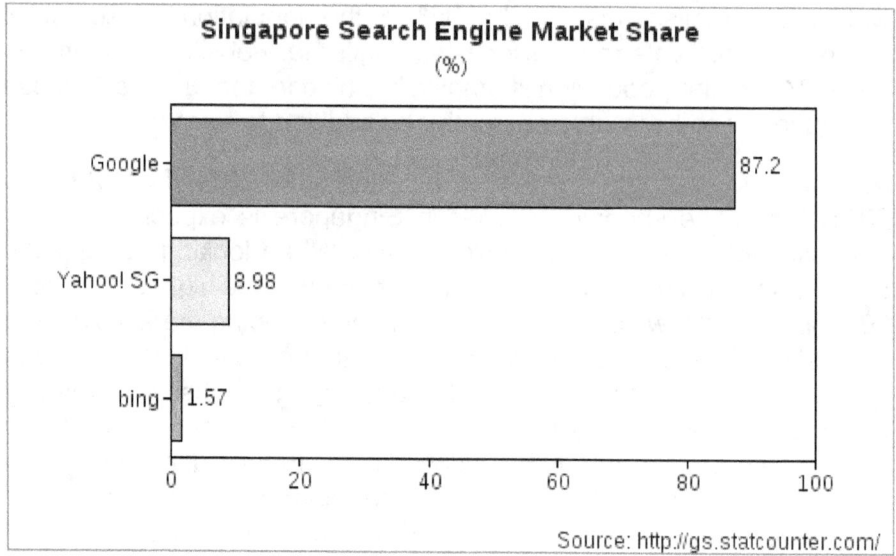

Fig 10.1.1: Overall search engine shares in Singapore

Google Singapore has a four-language interface (English, Simplified Chinese, Malay, and Tamil), so searches can and are being done in each one.

Fig 10.1.2: On Google Singapore, you can select up to 4 languages for your search.

The second most used search engine in Singapore is Yahoo! Singapore. Its interface only supports English, though.

Fig 10.1.3: Yahoo! Singapore—English is the only supported language in its interface.

PPC Advertising in Singapore

Because Google's share of the search engine market in Singapore is the highest by far, PPC marketing is done predominantly through Google AdWords. According to 2011 research conducted by comScore, in Singapore there was a total of approximately 304 million searches per month, which amounted to an average of 115 searches a month per person. As previously mentioned, there are four major languages spoken in Singapore, so it is imperative to choose which language you would like to target when developing and marketing your website. We naturally recommend using Google AdWords' keyword tool to research search volumes as an initial step of your marketing research, as it will reveal the reach of your potential market. Many corporations are search engine marketing in English or Simplified Chinese, which means there is less competition in the Malaysian and Tamil language online markets.

Singaporean SEO

Because Google's share of the search engine market is so high in Singapore, SEO should be performed with Google's algorithms in mind. Google's search engine algorithms are universal, regardless of country, so naturally your site's SEO should mirror that of any other country's Google-based SEO strategy. This means you will need solid internal and external SEO. Of course, when you develop link building strategies, it's recommended to use domestic sites or those with .sg domains as the links are more effective.

Search Engine Directories in Singapore

+ http://www.thegreenbook.com/
+ http://www.yellowpages.com.sg

The Thai Online Market

		Reference
Population	64,377,000	IMF-World Economic Outlook Database 2012
Internet population	17,059,000	World Bank 2012
Internet use	26.5%	
Scale of online advertising market	2 billion THB	Digital Advertising Association of Thailand 2011

- 75% of the Internet community in Thailand is under 35 years old (comScore).
- Thai Internet users spend an average of 27 hours online per month (comScore).
- 96% of Internet users participate in social media (comScore).

Thailand's Internet community is comprised of 17,059,000 persons, which is only 26.5% of the population. The share that online advertising holds of Thailand's total advertising market is only about 2.1%. It is clear that the Internet and online marketing in Thailand are really just getting started.

The Thai Search Engine Market

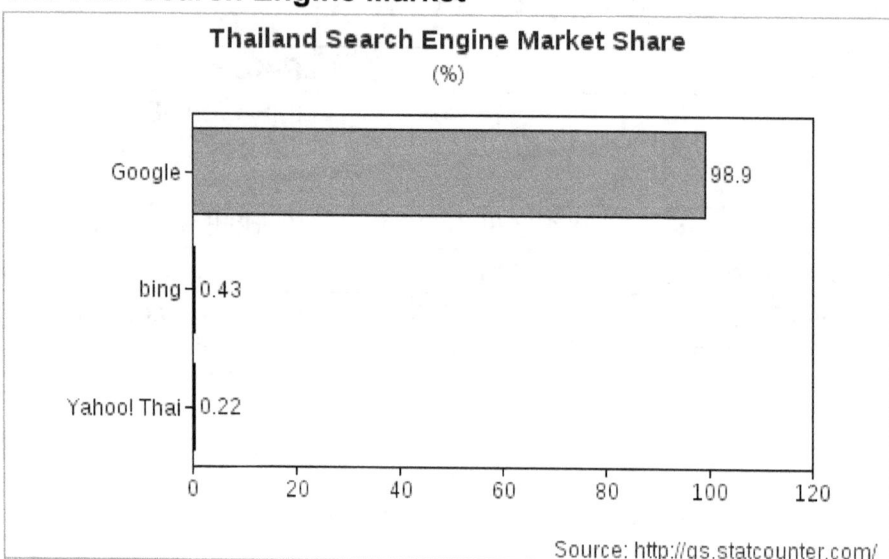

Fig 10.2.1: Overall search engine shares in Thailand

As the graph above illustrates, Google has captured nearly the entire Thai search engine market at 98.9%. Bing and Yahoo! combined don't even amount to 1%.

PPC Advertising in Thailand

By search engine marketing on Google, you will be able to reach nearly all of Thailand's search engine users. When planning your keywords and ad copy for your campaigns, it's important to have native speakers do it so that you will not lose any of the extensive reach you can capture in Thailand.

Thai SEO

In Thailand, there really isn't a strong understanding of how important SEO is for the promotion of a business's website. This is because Thailand's SEM market is still underdeveloped, when compared to that of its neighboring Asian countries. As a consequence, there isn't a great source of Thai-oriented information on SEO to reference. However, since Google is Thailand's main search engine (by far), it is best to generally tailor your SEO to suit Google's algorithms. For link building, as Thailand's SEO industry is still significantly small in scale, developing an extensive and diverse portfolio can be challenging. One positive point about Thai SEO, though, is that the online market is not flooded with sites (as is the West) and so there are fewer to compete against for ranking. If you were to be one of the first sites to optimize for Google, you could position your site to gain more traffic than your competitors.

Search Engine Directories in Thailand

- http://www.thaiwebsites.com/
  Registration page: http://www.thaiwebsites.com/submitwebsite.htm

- http://dir.sanook.com/
  Registration page: http://dir.sanook.com/addweb/

The Vietnamese Online Market

		Reference
Population	90,388,000	IMF–World Economic Outlook Database 2012
Internet population	35,703,000	World Bank 2012
Internet use	39.5%	
Scale of online advertising market	27.0 milllion USD	Vietnam Advertising Association 2011

- It is estimated that Vietnam's Internet population will reach 58,000,000 by the year 2016 (EIU).
- 95% of Vietnamese aged 15-24 are avid Internet users (Cimigo NetCitizens 2012).
- News is the main reason Vietnamese access the Internet, followed by general searches, music, research, and online chat (Cimigo).
- Internet users in Vietnam spend an average of 16 hours per week online (Nielsen).
- 58% of the Internet population in Vietnam researches a product it is interested in buying before it makes a purchase (VCCI).
- 97% of 15-24 year old Vietnamese participate in social media (We Are Social).

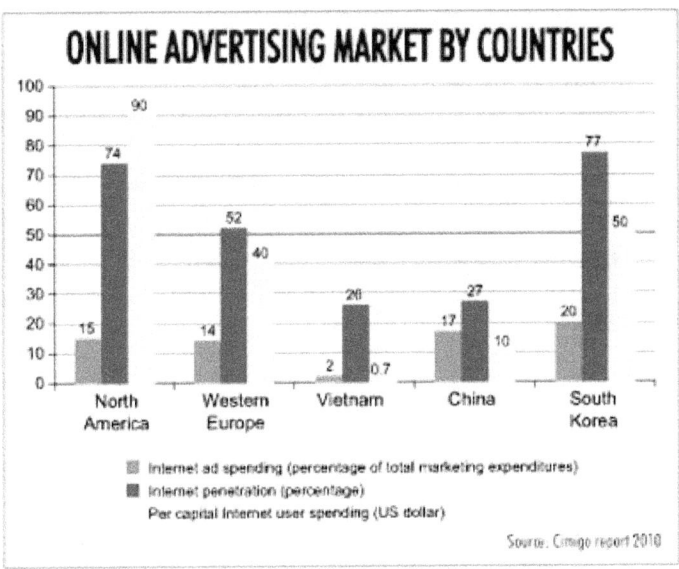

Fig 10.3.1: The price of online advertising in Vietnam is low compared to other markets.

In a 2011 investigation by Kanter Media, it was found that online advertising in Vietnam was only 3.5% of the entire Vietnamese advertising market. While this figure is undoubtedly low, the scale of the market is expected to grow as the number of Internet users in Vietnam increases, just as in other Asian countries.

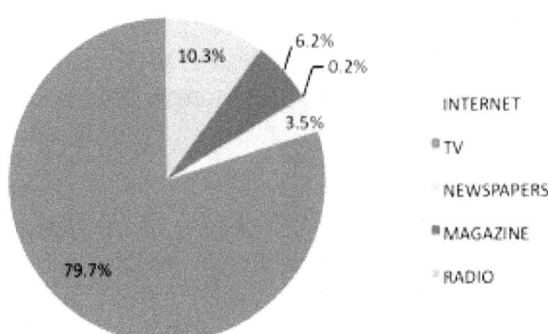

Fig 10.3.2: A comparison of the various advertising forms in Vietnam, where in the share of online advertising is only 3.5%
Source: http://ads.zing.vn/blogs/blog/10/Online-trends-in-Vietnam

The Vietnamese Search Engine Market

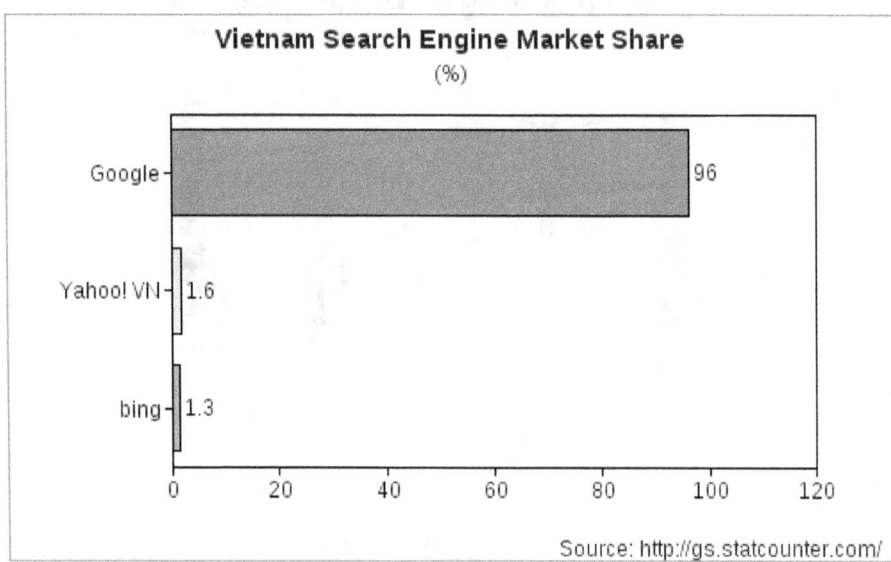

Fig 10.3.3: Overall search engine shares in Vietnam

As seen above, Google has been able to command an extremely large share of the Vietnamese search engine market.

PPC Advertising in Vietnam

As previously mentioned, the size of the entire Vietnamese online market is rather small, so the amount of advertising that is being done online is also very small. The good news is that it means there is less competition. If you are planning to target the Vietnamese online market, planning your integration now or the near future could be the best time. And, since Google has the highest share of the search engines, AdWords is the best platform to utilize.

When searching for the keyword "insurance" in Vietnam and in the Vietnamese language, there is a low level of competition with an equally low monthly search volume of 1,300. In Japan, however, there is a high level of competition and the monthly search volume is 49,500. Naturally the CPC in Vietnam is lower than in Japan, at an average 23 JPY (approx. $.23 USD).

Search terms		Avg. monthly searches ?	Competition ?	Suggested bid ?
bảo hiểm		1 300	Low	¥23

Fig 10.3.4: Monthly search volume, competition level and suggest bid price for "insurance" in Vietnam.

Search terms		Avg. monthly searches ?	Competition ?	Suggested bid ?
保険		49 500	High	¥961

Fig 10.3.5: Monthly search volume, competition level and suggest bid price for "insurance" in Japan.

Vietnamese SEO
Just as in other Asian countries, SEO needs to be performed in light of Google's search engine algorithms. As titles and meta tags will be shown in the Google search results, it is important to not only include relevant keywords with enough search volume, but also to write attractive titles and meta tags so that you can capture a good amount of traffic. With regard to backlinks, since there are relatively few sites in Vietnam that can be used for building your link portfolio, it is recommended you submit your site's URL to directories, such as the one below.

Search Engine Directories in Vietnam
- http://wada.vn/
- http://vn.yahoo.com/
- http://www.viet.net/

The Indonesian Online Market

		Reference
Population	244,468,000	IMF-World Economic Outlook Database 2012
Internet population	37,648,000	World Bank 2012
Internet use	15.4%	
Scale of online advertising market	40 million USD	Jakarta Update 2011

- The online advertising market in Indonesia will grow to 150 million USD by the year 2016 (Jakarta Update 2011).
- The number of Facebook users in Indonesia in November 2012 was measured at 50,261,100. This placed Indonesia fourth in the world, behind only America (168,742,860), Brazil (62,240,840), and India (60,843,200) (Social Bakers).
- Broadband use in Indonesia was measured at 6% in 2011. It is estimated that this figure will grow to 60% by the year 2016 (Frost & Sullivan).
- 50% of Internet users in Indonesia are under 20 years old (We Are Social).

The number of Internet users in Indonesia has increased rapidly since 2009. In two years' time (from 2009 to 2011), this number grew 270%. In terms of Internet access, most users (57%) in Indonesia connect via mobile devices, as opposed to PCs (Nielsen). And, one interesting characteristic about Internet use in Indonesia is that Internet cafes are still quite popular. In fact, a report by Nielsen shows that more than half of the online population in Indonesia (66%) accesses the web from Internet cafes.

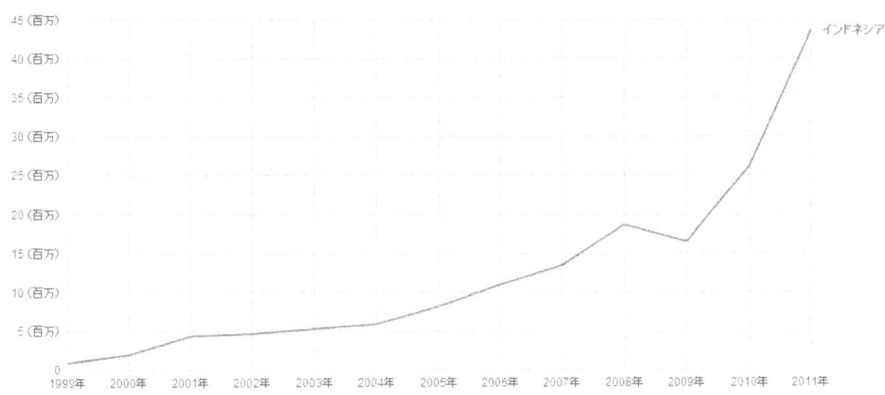

Fig 10.4.1: The increase in number of Internet users in Indonesia

As the graph above shows, since 2009, this number has risen rapidly. Yet, compared to other Asian countries, Indonesia's increase in broadband use is low. This is the next issue Internet users in Indonesia will face.

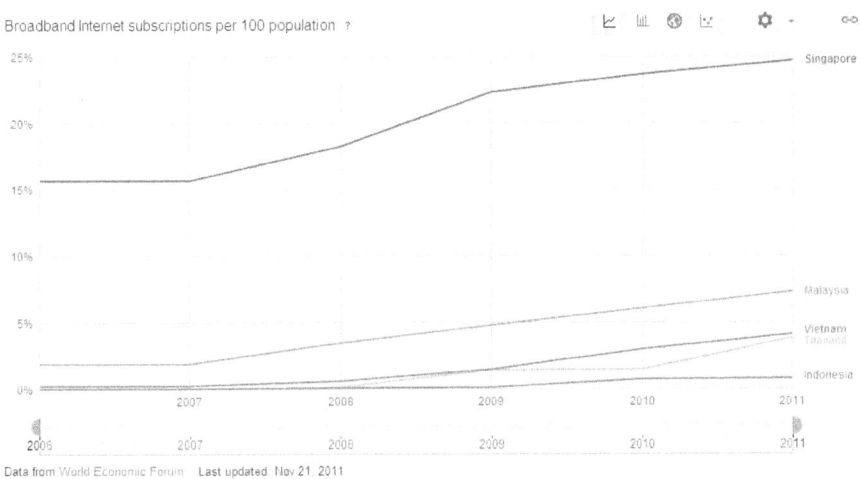

Fig 10.4.2: Number of broadband Internet users per 100 individuals

As you can see, Indonesia's figures are lower than its neighboring Southeast Asian countries.

The Indonesian Search Engine Market

Fig 10.4.3: Overall search engine shares in Indonesia

Just like in most other Southeast Asian countries, Google commands the top share of the search engine market.

PPC Advertising in Indonesia

Since Google commands the top share of the Indonesian search engine market, advertising online in Indonesia is best done through Google AdWords. However, the percentage of mobile Internet access in Indonesia is high, and Google is not always the preferred search engine on mobile devices. Yahoo! can command a higher traffic rate depending on the keywords searched. Since there is a large amount of Internet access through mobile devices, it is safe to say that it is good idea to run mobile campaigns on both AdWords and Yahoo!.

While Indonesia does have a surprisingly high number of English speakers within the population, naturally, it isn't spoken as much as the country's native language; therefore, for SEM campaigns, the Indonesian language is recommended. For instance, consider a search for the keyword "airline ticket" in English and Indonesian. It becomes clear that the disparity between the two in terms of searches per month is significant: For English there are only 110 monthly searches, but for Indonesian, as many as 165,000.

Keyword (by relevance)	Avg. monthly searches ?	Competition ?
airline ticket	110	High

Fig 10.4.4: Monthly search volume for "airline ticket"

Keyword (by relevance)	Avg. monthly searches ?	Competition ?
tiket pesawat	165.000	High

Fig 10.4.5: Monthly search volume for "tiket pesawat"

Google AdWords allows for PPC advertising in both English and Indonesian; however, it is not recommended that you use Indonesian keywords for an English language landing page (or vice versa). The problem is that your ads can stop in certain instances and there will be an overall disconnect between the service/product the Indonesian search user is looking for and what he ends up finding at the end of his or her journey.

Indonesian SEO

For Indonesia, SEO should naturally target Google, as it is the most widely used search engine. However, as mentioned above, Yahoo! does command significant traffic for mobile device use, so considering mobile SEO for Yahoo! is also recommended. One important point about Yahoo!, though, is that it is now powered by Bing. This means that Yahoo! Indonesia and Bing Indonesia will provide identical search results, and in terms of SEO for Yahoo!, you must do everything in accordance with Bing's algorithms.

Search Engine Directories in Indonesia

* http://id.yahoo.com/

About Rohan Yamagishi

Japanese native, piano lover, and Asian digital marketing expert, Rohan Yamagishi, recognized early on that while the Internet has made the world a smaller place in many ways, there are still great differences in culture and language nuances between the East and the West. It was from this realization that Rohan decided he would start his own business to help companies who were struggling to sell their products and services in Asia. And, it was search engine marketing that Rohan believed would be the best means of doing so.

After graduating from Minnesota State University Mankato with a degree in Computer Information Science, Rohan quickly made the move to start up his own search engine marketing company. First starting in America, he eventually realized that his company would run better if located in Japan. In 2004, Rohan mad the move back to his native country with his company, Info Cubic Japan. As CEO, Rohan has had the great opportunity to meet many great people and help a multitude of foreign and domestic companies, of all sizes and industries, expand their business throughout the continent of Asia.

About Paul Tarpey (Translator and Editor)

American-born Japanese language translator, Paul Tarpey, has a rich background in translating various online and offline texts from the Japanese to the English language. Some of his core work involves content from the manufacturing and marketing sectors.

After receiving his Master of Arts degree in Applied Linguistics at San Diego State University, Paul quickly made the decision to move to Japan and start a new career in online marketing, an industry he had developed a great interest in through his translation work.

Since moving to Japan and joining the team at Info Cubic Japan, a digital marketing agency in the heart of Tokyo, Paul has not only been able to continue his work translating various online content, but also has gained much experience in the field of search engine marketing. Currently, Paul is working as a multilingual SEM consultant, wherein he provides bilingual services to clients from all across the world.

About Info Cubic Japan

Info Cubic Japan is Asia's premiere SEM firm, focusing on paid and organic search engine marketing, social media and media buying services for the APAC region. Starting his company in America over a decade ago and moving back with his business to Japan, CEO, Rohan Yamagishi, has had the great opportunity to assist countless corporations looking to expand their business across Asia. Using the most recent tools and up-to-date market research, Info Cubic Japan has been able to grow itself 150% year-over-year. And, in order to serve clients from all across the East and the West more effectively, Info Cubic Japan has employed in-house native speakers of Chinese, Korean and English, all of whom are online marketing professionals. With Info Cubic Japan as your partner, you can be confident you are joining a team of professionals on the cutting-edge of today's and tomorrow's leading online marketing practices for the Asian market.

Company website: http://www.infocubic.co.jp/en/

-

www.ingramcontent.com/pod-product-compliance
Lightning Source LLC
LaVergne TN
LVHW021129190326
834317LV00008B/237